Suburbia

A GUIDE TO INFORMATION SOURCES

Volume 9 in the Urban Studies Information Guide Series

Joseph Zikmund II

Associate Professor of Political Science

and

Chairman of the Social Science Department
Illinois Institute of Technology
Chicago

Deborah Ellis Dennis

Research Associate and Librarian
Social Research Group
George Washington University
Washington, D.C.

Gale Research Company
Book Tower, Detroit, Michigan 48226

Library of Congress Cataloging in Publication Data

Zikmund, Joseph.
  Suburbia.

  (Urban studies information guide series ; v. 9)
  Bibliography: p. 142
  Includes indexes.
  1. Suburbs--Bibliography.   2. Suburban life--
Bibliography.   I. Dennis, Deborah Ellis, joint
author.   II. Title.   III. Series.
Z7164.U7Z54   [HT371]   016.30136'2   78-10523
ISBN 0-8103-1435-5

Suburbia

URBAN STUDIES INFORMATION GUIDE SERIES

Series Editor: Thomas P. Murphy, Director, Institute for Urban Studies at the University of Maryland, College Park (on leave) and Director of the Federal Executive Institute, Charlottesville, Virginia

Also in this series:

URBAN COMMUNITY—*Edited by Anthony J. Filipovitch and Earl J. Reeves*

URBAN DECISION MAKING: THE BASIS FOR ANALYSIS—*Edited by Mark Drucker**

URBAN EDUCATION—*Edited by George E. Spear and Donald W. Mocker*

URBAN FISCAL POLICY AND ADMINISTRATION—*Edited by John L. Mikesell and Jerry L. McCaffery**

URBAN HOUSING: PUBLIC AND PRIVATE—*Edited by John E. Rouse, Jr.*

URBAN INDICATORS—*Edited by Thomas P. Murphy**

URBAN LAW—*Edited by Thomas P. Murphy**

URBAN MANAGEMENT—*Edited by Bernard H. Ross*

URBAN PLANNING—*Edited by Ernest R. Alexander, Anthony J. Catanese, and David S. Sawicki*

URBAN POLICY—*Edited by Dennis J. Palumbo and George Taylor*

URBAN POLITICS—*Edited by Thomas P. Murphy*

WOMEN AND URBAN SOCIETY—*Edited by Hasia R. Diner*

*in preparation

The above series is part of the
GALE INFORMATION GUIDE LIBRARY

The Library consists of a number of separate series of guides covering major areas in the social sciences, humanities, and current affairs.

General Editor: Paul Wasserman, Professor and former Dean, School of Library and Information Services, University of Maryland

Managing Editor: Denise Allard Adzigian, Gale Research Company

VITAE

Joseph Zikmund II is presently an associate professor of political science and chairman of the social science department at Illinois Institute of Technology in Chicago. He received his B.A. degree from Beloit College, Wisconsin; his M.S. degree from the University of Wisconsin-Madison; and a Ph.D. in political science from Duke University, North Carolina. In addition to numerous published articles and monographs, Zikmund has written READING GUIDE IN POLITICS AND GOVERNMENT and ECOLOGY OF AMERICAN POLITICAL CULTURE. He is a member of the American Political Science Association and the Midwest Political Science Association. He is presently the book review editor of PUBLIUS.

Deborah Ellis Dennis is presently a research associate and librarian with the social research group at George Washington University in Washington, D.C. She received a B.S.J. degree from Northwestern University and an A.M. degree from the University of Chicago. Dennis compiled and edited the ANNUAL REPORT for the Center for Urban Affairs, nos. 4-8, and coauthored with Louis H. Masotti, SUBURBS, SUBURBIA AND SUBURBANIZATION: A BIBLIOGRAPHY, 2d ed. She belongs to the American Library Association, Special Libraries Association, and Society of Professional Journalists-Sigma Delta Chi.

CONTENTS

Contents

PREFACE

This is a book whose time is long overdue. For those of us who have labored in the vast, uncharted terrain of suburban literature in the past, this volume would have been invaluable, as it will be for those who will do so hereafter.

Simply attempting to survey the diverse and extensive literature which purports to be "suburban" is a herculean task, as Hadden, Dennis, and I discovered when we published two editions of the SUBURBS, SUBURBIA AND SUBURBANIZATION bibliography a few years ago. Actually reading and annotating that literature and then establishing meaningful and useful categories for it is an activity which boggles the mind. And yet, that is precisely what Zikmund and Dennis have done so effectively in this volume of the Gale Urban Studies Information Guide Series. It should have an immediate and lasting influence on suburban research as a result of both its content and its organization.

Suburban scholars, public officials, and thoughtful suburban citizens and groups owe a heavy debt to the compilers of this research guide.

Louis H. Masotti, Director
Center for Urban Affairs
Northwestern University
Evanston, Illinois

INTRODUCTION

The suburbs contain about 40 percent of our population and are at the center of many of our most serious social issues. Much is assumed and much is asserted about suburbia, the people who live there, and the politics which emerges as a result. Yet, the amount of good social science research focused on these people and their ways of living is certainly not proportional to their numbers or their importance. Scholarship tends to concentrate on the urban not the suburban, on the upper and lower classes not on those in the middle, on the deviant and the extraordinary not the typical and routine. There is a significant professional literature on suburbs, suburbanites, and suburbia--as this volume will demonstrate. But in many ways what strikes the person who surveys this literature with care is how little we know, not how much. Many of the vital studies are ten to twenty years old; they are dated. Much of the data is from selected communities, metropolitan areas or regions; its relevance may not be universal. As suburbia becomes larger, the opportunities it provides for serious research expand. Thus far scholarly productivity has not matched the suburban phenomenon. All too much of the suburban literature is fugitive, faddish, and doctrinaire. The literature on suburbia may be described as fugitive in at least two distinct ways, and unquestionably this has affected the character of this book. Traditionally, we call a body of literature fugitive when it is hard to locate and, as a result, difficult to use. Our search for the items to be annotated here has made it quite clear that a good deal of the material is hard to find. In fact, some has been so fugitive that we were not able to locate it at all. Books are from small presses; articles appear in journals with very limited circulation. Occasionally even major university libraries are not sufficient. We have had our troubles, and we expect that some of the selections we found and annotated may prove difficult for others to locate. If the best material were the easiest to find, we would have little concern, but this is not necessarily the case.

As troublesome as it is to find the suburban literature at times, it seems to be even more of a problem to know what to look for. Put simply, some of what is labeled "suburban" really is not, and some of what would appropriately fit is not so identified. Early in this enterprise we decided to limit our scope to those items which were suburban qua suburban. That is, we wished to emphasize the literature which is, so to speak, purely suburban, not metropolitan, not urban. This is one of the reasons why the body of literature annotated in this book is not large. We have chosen to emphasize those items which focus primarily on suburbia or suburban people and phenomena. Many studies have been done in suburbia which do not explicitly emphasize or even recognize the unique suburban elements in their setting. Sometimes these are entitled "suburban" although it is difficult or impossible to discern any special suburban concern whatsoever. For the most part, if there is not a clearly identifiable suburban aspect to the study, we have not included it no matter what the title may say. By contrast, there are numerous works which are definitely suburban, in the sense we mean it, that are not so labeled by the author (and thus often are missed by periodical indexing services). Undoubtedly, we also have missed some of these items. We hope the number is small. In sum, as careful and thorough as we have tried to be, unquestionably there are items of relevance which have not been annotated for this volume.

Our second assertion about the suburban literature is that it is faddish. Studies of suburbia vary dramatically in their subject matter from era to era. In the 1940s and 1950s, primary attention focused on the character of suburbia. Was there "community" in suburbia? Was suburbia a degregation of traditional urban life and values--neither urban nor rural and reflecting the worst of each? Suburban case studies were common. The suburban society, the suburban myth, and the organization man all came under intense investigation, and the scholarly debate over the true character of suburbia was genuine and serious. Suburban politics--or more accurately, the impact of suburbanization on American national politics and especially presidential elections--also was subject to close scrutiny. Not since 1967 has there been a full-scale suburban case study which sought to understand the community rather than contribute to the debate on some contemporary social issue. The era of general suburban community studies seems for the time being to have passed. During the 1960s the literature on suburbia turned metropolitan. Metropolitanism and the interaction between central cities and suburbs came to the fore. In the 1970s, two interrelated concerns have monopolized scholars' attention: (1) the impact of suburban growth on urban problems, particularly central city public finance, and (2) race, zoning, and--as one writer puts it--the politics of exclusion.

All of these are important questions worthy of concentrated attention. However, they do not add up to a full body of knowledge about suburbia. We still have no well-tested theory of suburbanization, its impact on suburban residents, its patterns of politics, its consequences for social institutions. We know a great deal about some things, but very little about others. The literature is spotty and incomplete, a condition at least partly a product of the faddishness of social science concern with the suburbs. When a special topic gets "hot," volumes of material appear; when the same topic "cools," interest turns to other matters. Perhaps this is a problem in much of social science. Perhaps it is a problem with all of modern science. The consequences in this area of study has been to generate a body of literature as diverse as suburbia itself. It does not hang together; rather it is a little theory here

and an empirical study there. Given the increasing importance of suburbia
to American life, we ought to have more systematic knowledge than we do
at present.

Finally, we assert that too much of the suburban literature presents a doctrinaire or subjectively biased picture of suburbia. Although this is not true of
all or even most of the professional social science books and articles written
about suburbia, it is clear that many authors have found it very difficult to
be neutral about their suburban subject matter. The tendency is to make social evaluation an integral part of otherwise serious empirical research. Suburbia, for whatever reasons, seems to provoke judgment. Personal preferences,
of course, are inevitable, but when these preferences pass for serious scholar-
ship--pro or con--genuine understanding suffers. Just why the suburbs produce
this reaction in intellectuals is a question beyond the scope of this introduction. In any case, we can say that the contentious character of this portion
of the suburban literature makes finding out what really goes on beyond the
central city boundaries considerably more difficult. Not only must readers
find something relevant to their interests, but they must also wade through
the emotions and personal prejudgments of the author as well. For some, it
is easier to like or dislike suburbia than it is to understand it.

THE BOOK

Our observations about the suburban literature have influenced the composition
of this annotated bibliography. A quick glance at the table of contents or
a flip through the pages will make it clear to the reader that the book is
organized topically. As a reference tool, we have assumed that most users
will be looking for citations regarding some particular subject. We have
grouped the books, articles, and chapters on the basis of their own emphases.
Similarly, we have kept the categories broad, assuming that some materials
could fit more than one place and that most readers are likely to be seeking
the literature on housing, for example, rather than just the one or two items
on urban renewal projects sponsored by regional organizations in the suburbs.

The one major exception to this general organizational structure of the bibliography is our treatment of the readers, edited collections, and special journal issues, which we have listed separately in a section by themselves. Their
numbers are relatively small, and the researcher usually has convenient access
to them all through university or major public libraries. At the same time,
paradoxically, had we tried to annotate each separate, original contribution
in these volumes, the size of this book would have increased by more than
50 percent. As a practical compromise, we have listed the titles of all such
contributions under the particular book, but have annotated only the collection as a whole. As a result, the reader is advised to check the contents
of the readers no matter what subject matter is being explored.

Introduction

Two further comments are in order concerning the contents of this bibliography. The original design of the project called for including only material published after 1965. For the most part we have stuck to that plan. However, it soon became apparent that a number of crucial selections--especially books-- appeared before that date. As a result, we modified our intentions in order to include the most relevant books and a few classic articles which came into print before 1965.

We also decided to eliminate certain classes of materials. Virtually all of the contentious, journalistic discussion appearing in popular mass circulation periodicals has been omitted. While these materials may give some indication of the tone and character of the debate over suburbia at any particular time, they add little to our knowledge of suburbia itself. Doctoral dissertations have not been included because they are well indexed in DISSERTATION ABSTRACTS INTERNATIONAL and, more importantly, because they usually find their way into books and journal articles. The decision was also made to confine our search to readily available materials, thus excluding most government documents, occasional papers published by university departments, and other ephemera.

Finally, recognizing that some readers will be seeking access to the suburban literature for purposes other than the substantive topics explored by these studies, we have provided three distinct indexes to the annotations. First, we have an index of all authors cited. Second is a list of all book titles referenced. Third, we provide a geographical index based on the metropolitan area on which the research focuses. Here we have listed only those studies which concentrate on just one or two metropolitan areas. Thus, perhaps as much as 50 percent of the items annotated are not included in the geographical index. These either have no particular geographical focus, are national in scope, or take in so many different SMSAs as to dilute greatly the attention given to any one area.

I. GENERAL

A. BOOKS

1   Donaldson, Scott. THE SUBURBAN MYTH. New York: Columbia University Press, 1969.

Donaldson's book is a milestone in the history of the study of American suburbs. In it the author looks back over several decades of suburban research and literary treatment and tries to explain why the "suburban myth" developed, what encouraged the myth during the 1950s, and what weaknesses exist in this stereotyped approach to the suburbs.

Reaching back to the early part of the twentieth century, Donaldson reviews early commentaries on suburbia and classifies the antisuburban literature into several distinct categories. In the process, the writings of Douglass, Riesman, Mumford, Whyte, and Wright are examined. An underlying thread, Donaldson argues, is the persistence of the Jeffersonian ideal in American culture and intellectual history. By being neither city nor country, the suburbs catch it from both sides; they are not rural enough to embody the truly agrarian, Jeffersonian ideal, nor are they urban enough to fulfill the expectations of supporters of big cities. A little bit of everything but nothing unique or distinct, the suburbs are damned from all sides.

In response to the myth Donaldson outlines the findings of Berger, Dobriner, and others emphasizing suburban diversity. For the most part, Donaldson relies on critical analysis and the juxtaposing of contradictory studies rather than his own new data or empirical research.

A major contribution to the intellectual history of suburbs.

2   Muller, Peter O. THE OUTER CITY. Association of American Geographers Resource Paper no. 75-2. Washington, D.C.: 1976.

An excellent work on the American city. In 54 pages Muller

1

has provided a very good summary of the professional literature on suburbia. The history of American suburbia, spatial organization in suburbia, issues of suburban exclusion, and the changing role of suburbs in American metropolitan areas all are considered and effectively presented. This is an important statement of the state of suburbia and suburbanology in 1976.

3   Murphy, Thomas P., and Rehfuss, John. URBAN POLITICS IN THE SUB-URBAN ERA. Homewood, Ill.: Dorsey Press, 1976.

From the title and preface it is somewhat difficult to discern that this book is an introductory text on suburban local government. The first chapter on suburban growth provides excellent background material on suburbia. Other chapters on suburban power, suburban government and politics, types of suburbs, and similar topics adequately introduce the student to the main themes of these areas. At times there appears to be some confusion between the discussion of suburban patterns versus local government in general. However, this is an extremely useful addition to the suburban literature, an item which is likely to dominate the suburban text market for some time.

4   Sobin, Dennis P. THE FUTURE OF THE AMERICAN SUBURBS. Port Washington, N.Y.: Kennikat Press, 1971.

In a generally negative overview, Sobin provides a useful review of the book literature--especially the critical, journalistic literature--on suburbia. The question which the author poses is: Can the suburbs survive? After illustrating the existence of industrial suburbs and suburban slums, Sobin explores why suburbia has attracted so many new residents. He argues that suburbia is an artificial creation with an unnatural separation from the central city, that there are real social problems inherent in suburbia and that the forces which brought people to suburbia and keep them there are rapidly disappearing. Sobin concludes that the old-style suburbia cannot survive--surbuban new towns and urbanized older suburbs will be the suburbia of the future.

5   Wirt, Frederick M.; Walter, Benjamin; Rabinovitz, Francine F.; and Hensler, Deborah R. ON THE CITY'S RIM. Lexington, Mass.: D.C. Heath, 1972.

The first attempt since Wood's SUBURBIA (see item 6) to provide a comprehensive picture of suburbia and suburban politics. Parts 1, 2, and 4, entitled "History and Social Demography," "Electoral Behavior," and "Local Political Conflict," are written by Wirt and Benjamin Walter. Part 3, entitled "The Suburban State of Mind," is by Deborah R. Hensler; the last part, "National

Policy Problems," is by Francine F. Rabinovitz. Because of the special interests of the several authors, the book makes lasting, original contributions in the areas of suburban voting, suburban attitudes, and the impact of national public policy on the suburbs.

ON THE CITY'S RIM is a major addition to the suburban literature. It is readily available in paperback for classroom as well as scholarly use.

6   Wood, Robert C. SUBURBIA. Boston: Houghton Mifflin, 1958.

As the author notes in his preface, this is a different kind of critique of suburbia--at least the suburbia of the 1950s. This is not the blistering indictment of mass culture at mid-century nor is it a purveyor of the unidimensional stereotype. Wood understands the complexity and diversity of American suburbia and does not succumb to doctrinaire rejection. The author's criticisms of suburbia derive from careful analyses of what suburbia is and what the needs of America are in our time.

An important contribution of the book appears in the section on suburban politics. Here, as elsewhere, Wood sorts out the theories of the times (late 1950s) and gives coherence to the academic arguments at that point. His discussions of the suburban boss, nonpartisanship, school politics, and other local issues remain today original and useful parts of the suburban literature. A major classic for students of American suburbia.

B. ARTICLES

7   Berger, Bennett M. "Suburbia and the American Dream." PUBLIC IN-TEREST, no. 2, Winter 1966, pp. 80-91.

Berger attempts to relate the accumulated research on suburbs to some of the more pervasive pluralisms of American culture and then to some problems of planning for urban diversity. The author attributes the persistence of the myth of suburbia to the fit between the description of suburbia and the prescriptive desires of every opinion from right to left. The myth is profoundly related to American ambivalence about cultural pluralism. Berger foresees three alternatives for planning the quality and culture of urban life: (1) planning for the cultural context beyond family solidarity, (2) altering the environments of certain groups in order to improve their culture, a policy Berger feels would founder on its utopian idealism, and (3) planning for a pluralist society, the alternative he recommends.

8   Beyer, Glenn H. "Suburbia." In HOUSING AND SOCIETY, edited by
     Glenn H. Beyer, pp. 358-86. New York: Macmillan, 1965.

     General introduction to suburbanization and the suburban lit-
     erature up to 1965.

9   Fava, Sylvia [Fleis]. "The Pop Sociology of Suburbs and New Towns."
     AMERICAN STUDIES (U. of Kans.) 14 (Spring 1973): 121.

     Fava defines "pop sociology," practiced in the mass media and
     used in conventional wisdom, as stereotyped, unscientific,
     ideological, oversimplified, instant, all-encompassing, and
     superficial. Suburbia maintains its image in pop sociology
     despite scholarly findings to the contrary because of Americans'
     adherence to the myth of homogeneity, their inability to deal
     with pluralism, and their alleged preference for rural life.
     The author finds that new towns have now become the primary
     focus of pop sociology, which is generally favorable to the
     idea but still largely descriptive and hortatory despite the ex-
     plicit federal policies and concerns with social issues.

10   Hadden, Jeffrey K. "Use of Ad Hoc Definitions." In SOCIOLOGICAL
     METHODOLOGY, edited by Edgar F. Borgatta, pp. 276-85. San Fran-
     cisco: Jossey-Bass, 1968.

     Critical examination of the concept of "suburb." Illustrates
     the difficulties with various Census Bureau definitions and their
     implications for alternative research strategies. Author sug-
     gests that "suburbia" can rest within the political boundaries
     of the central city and that not all places outside those polit-
     ical boundaries ought to be considered suburban.

11   Hall, Peter. "The Urban Culture and the Suburban Culture." In MAN
     IN THE CITY OF THE FUTURE, edited by Richard Eells and Clarence
     Walton, pp. 99-145. Toronto: Collier-Macmillan Canada, 1968.

     General review of suburban literature which emphasizes how
     suburbs have been treated in the urban studies and planning
     literature.

12   Schiltz, Timothy, and Moffitt, William. "Inner-City/Outer-City Rela-
     tionships in Metropolitan Areas." URBAN AFFAIRS QUARTERLY 7 (Sep-
     tember 1971): 75-108.

     A lengthy bibliographic essay covering much of the suburban
     literature published to that time. The authors put primary em-
     phasis, however, on those materials directed to city-suburban
     contrasts and interactive relationships. Among the topics cov-
     ered are central city-suburban disparities, governmental frag-
     mentation, and metropolitanism. A long bibliography of sources
     is included.

13   Wood, Robert C. "The American Suburb." In MAN AND THE MODERN
      CITY, edited by Elizabeth Geen et al., pp. 112-21. Pittsburgh: Uni-
      versity of Pittsburgh Press, 1963.

         Wood, in a very tightly reasoned and well-written essay, argues
         that suburbs result from three fundamental American values--the
         economic profit motive, the ongoing community (or neighbor-
         hood) manifestations of social class, and the concern for small-
         scale government. The author argues that our changing needs
         in urban America require that we seek new and different con-
         cepts of community and government to counter the negative
         aspects of suburbanization.

14   Wrong, Dennis H. "Suburbs and Myths of Suburbia." In READINGS IN
      INTRODUCTORY SOCIOLOGY, edited by Dennis H. Wrong and H.L.
      Gracey, pp. 358-64. New York: Macmillan, 1967.

         General review of the literature on suburbia. Special atten-
         tion is paid to the "myth of suburbia," its origins, its evolu-
         tion, and its weaknesses. Article ends with affirmations of
         suburban diversity and the oneness of the "urbanization" and
         "suburbanization" process.

C. READERS AND COLLECTIONS OF ESSAYS

15   Baker, Earl M., ed. "The Suburban Reshaping of American Politics."
      PUBLIUS 5 (Winter 1975): entire issue.

         This collection of original essays grew out of a conference at
         Temple University as part of the Toward '76 series sponsored
         by the Center for the Study of Federalism. Although the ar-
         ticles overlap occasionally, there is no dominant central theme
         to the collection; each author reports on his own research or
         summarizes his own area of substantive interest.

         The chapters may be divided roughly into three categories,
         based on the primary emphasis in each selection: theoretical,
         empirical, and review of summarizing contributions.

         In the first group can be placed Baker's introductory essay,
         "The Suburban Transformation of American Politics;" "The
         Politics of Urban Space" by Oliver P. Williams; and "Sub-
         urbanization: Reviving the Town on the Metropolitan Frontier"
         by Daniel J. Elazar. All three present some national or
         metropolitan area data to support their theoretical assertions.
         Three other articles are primarily empirical. "Eco-Policy En-
         vironment and Political Processes in 76 Cities of a Metropolitan
         Region" by Heinz Eulau and Kenneth Prewitt is an outgrowth
         of their study in the San Francisco Bay area and is similar to
         chapter 30 in their LABYRINTHS OF DEMOCRACY. David W.
         Scott contributed a case study of school district collaboration

entitled "Metropolitan Transaction Patterns in Suburban Chicago."
"Sources of the Suburban Population" by Joseph Zikmund II
explores the hypothesis that suburbia has been populated primarily by people moving from the central cities to the suburbs.
The final two selections in this collection--"Suburban Politics
and Policies" by Robert C. Wood, and "Suburbs and Politics
in America" by Frederick M. Wirt summarize aspects of the
existing state of suburban research.

Although the book is not a well integrated whole, several of
the pieces make important contributions to their specialized
areas.

16   Dobriner, William M., ed.   THE SUBURBAN COMMUNITY.   New York:
G.P. Putnam's Sons, 1958.

The first suburban reader, THE SUBURBAN COMMUNITY remains a classic and still-useful fixture in the literature on American suburbia. Of the twenty-five selections, about half are
original to this volume. Among these are the following:

>   Dobriner's introduction, "Theory and Research
>   in the Sociology of the Suburbs"
>   Fava, Sylvia [Fleis]. "Contrasts in Neighboring:
>   New York City and a Suburban Community"
>   Dobriner, William M. "Local and Cosmopolitan
>   as Contemporary Suburban Disaster Types"
>   Mowrer, Ernest R. "The Family in Suburbia"
>   Wood, Robert C. "The Governing of Suburbia"
>   Leonard, William N. "Economic Aspects of Sub-
>   urbanization"
>   Bell, Wendell. "Social Choice, Life Styles and
>   Suburban Residence"
>   Ennis, Philip H. "Leisure in the Suburbs: Research
>   Prolegomenon"
>   Meyersohn, Rolf, and Jackson, Robin. "Gardening
>   in Suburbia"
>   Wattel, Harold L. "Levittown: A Suburban Com-
>   munity"
>   Stonier, Charles E. "Problems of Suburban Trans-
>   port Services"
>   Fagin, Henry. "Problems of Planning in the Suburbs"
>   Riesman, David. "The Suburban Sadness"

17   Dolce, Philip C., ed.   SUBURBIA.   Garden City, N.Y.: Doubleday,
Anchor, 1976.

This collection of original essays on suburbia is primarily descriptive and interpretive. The volume gives an interdisci-
plinary perspective particularly suitable for students and the

general public. The individual pieces are listed below:

Schwartz, Joel. "The Evolution of the Suburbs"
Marsh, Margaret S., and Kaplan, Samuel. "The
  Lure of the Suburbs"
Wilkinson, Pierce B. "The Impact of Suburbaniza-
  tion on Government and Politics in Contemporary
  America"
Jackson, Kenneth T. "The Effect of Suburbaniza-
  tion on the Cities"
Vasiliadis, C.G. "The Arts and the Suburbs"
Davidoff, Paul, and Brooks, Richard [Oliver]. "Zon-
  ing Out the Poor"
Coppa, Frank J. "Cities and Suburbs in Europe
  and the United States"
Buder, Stanley. "The Future of American Suburbs"

Perhaps the most creative contributions are those by Schwartz,
who directly links suburbanization to Protestant-Catholic relations in the central cities, and by Vasiliadis, who explores
the varying patterns of interest in and support for the arts in
suburban communities.

18   Gans, Herbert J. PEOPLE AND PLANS. New York: Basic Books, 1968.

This collection of essays includes a number of previously published selections including "Urbanism and Suburbanism as Ways
of Life," "Planning and Social Life," and "The Balanced
Community." In addition there are four previously unpublished
pieces on suburbs: "The Suburban Community and Its Way of
Life," "Planning for the Everyday Life and Problems of Suburban and New Town Residents," "Suburbia Reclaimed," and
"The Disenchanted Suburbanite."

In sum, a good source for some of Gans's earlier, more fugitive thought on American suburbia.

19   Greer, Scott. THE URBANE VIEW. New York: Oxford University Press,
      1972.

THE URBANE VIEW is a collection of Greer's previously published articles with, for the most part, original introductions
to each of the book's four sections. Of interest to students
of suburbia are the following:

"Urbanism Reconsidered: A Comparative Study of
  Local Areas in a Metropolis"
"Urbanism and Social Structure"
"Dispersion and the Culture of Urban Man"
"Individual Participation in Mass Society"
"The Social Structure and Political Process of Sub-
  urbia - I"

"The Social Structure and Political Process of Sub-
   urbia - II: An Empirical Test"
"The Mass Society and the Parapolitical Structure"
"Dilemmas of Action Research on the Metropolitan
   Problem"
"The Rational Model, The Sociological Model, and
   Metropolitan Reform"
"Where is the Metropolitan Problem?"

As the titles indicate, a number of these deal with metropolitanism rather than suburbs as suburbs, and thus are marginal
to a purely suburban literature.

20   Haar, Charles M. SUBURBAN PROBLEMS. Cambridge, Mass.: Ballinger
      Publishing Co., 1974.

In October 1967, President Lyndon Johnson directed that a
national task force be created to study suburban problems.
The task force report, completed in the waning months of the
Johnson administration, profiled American suburbia and identified a number of existing problems as follows: (1) inflating
land costs; (2) abuse of the countryside and pollution; (3) increased transportation costs; (4) escalating home costs and the
exclusion of the disadvantaged; (5) psychological aimlessness;
and (6) increasing expense of public services and education.

Three major recommendations are put forth to cope with these
problems: first, creation of an Urban Development Bank to
open up new and larger sources of private and public capital
for public investment; second, development of a Federal
Urban Parklands Corporation to monitor and to control more
effectively urban land use; and third, housing assistance for
Vietnam veterans, the elderly, and other minorities to give
them better access to suburban living. Implicit in these recommendations is governmental and political change which
would allow metropolitan solutions to area-wide problems.

21   _____, ed. THE END OF INNOCENCE. Glenview, Ill.: Scott,
      Foresman, 1972.

A collection of popular and scholarly articles on suburbia.
More popular writers include Mumford, Moynihan, Fuller,
Wood, and Phillips. Several selections from the REPORT OF
THE PRESIDENT'S TASK FORCE ON SUBURBAN PROBLEMS
are included. Five of the articles appear for the first time
in this reader:

   McCausland, John. "Crime in the Suburbs"
   Cole, Leon Monroe. "Suburban Mobility"
   Campbell, Angus, and Schuman, Howard. "A Com-
      parison of Black and White Attitudes and Experi-
      ences in the City"

Aschmon, Frederick. "Accelerated Growth Centers"
Fuller, Buckminster. "Triton City"

22 Hughes, James W., ed. SUBURBAN DYNAMICS AND THE FUTURE OF
THE CITY. New Brunswick, N.J.: Rutgers University Press, 1974.

A collection of recent articles focusing on the processes of
suburbanization and the impact of suburbanization on blacks.
Original contributions include the introduction and Hughes's
"The Dynamics of Neighborhood Decline."

23 Kramer, John, ed. NORTH AMERICAN SUBURBS. Berkeley, Calif.:
Glendessary Press, 1972.

This paperback collection of both seminal and controversial
articles is obviously intended for classroom usage. Other than
Kramer's introduction, there are no selections original to this
volume. Among the general topics represented are the suburban myth, the changing character of suburbia, the diversity
both among and within suburbs, suburban politics, and the
future of suburbia. Nineteen articles and book chapters are
reproduced.

24 Masotti, Louis H., ed. "The Suburban Seventies." ANNALS OF THE
AMERICAN ACADEMY OF POLITICAL AND SOCIAL SCIENCE 422
(November 1975): 1-151.

A collection of essays which tries to break out of old patterns
and to open new areas of exploration. In some ways the
selections are speculative in character. This is an exciting
group of papers which tends to look ahead rather than back
to where suburban scholarship has been. The contents are as
follows:

Lineberry, Robert L. "Suburbia and the Metropoli-
tan Turf"
Fava, Sylvia F[leis]. "Beyond Suburbia"
Birch, David L. "From Suburb to Urban Place"
Scott, Thomas M. "Implications of Suburbanization
for Metropolitan Political Organization"
Zikmund, Joseph II. "A Theoretical Structure for
the Study of Suburban Politics"
Hughes, James W. "Dilemmas of Suburbanization
and Growth Controls"
Bradford, Calvin P., and Rubinowitz, Leonard S.
"The Urban-Suburban Investment-Disinvestment
Process: Consequences for Older Neighborhoods"
Taeuber, Karl E. "Racial Segregation: The Per-
sisting Dilemma"
Cataldo, Everett F.; Giles, Michael; and Gatlin,
Douglas. "Metropolitan School Desegregation:
Practical Remedy or Impractical Ideal?"

Steinlieb, George [S.], and Lake, Robert W. "Aging Suburbs and Black Homeownership"
Siembieda, William J. "Suburbanization of Ethnics of Color"
Smookler, Helene. "Administration Hara-Kiri: Implementation of the Urban Growth and New Community Development Act"
Lehne, Richard. "Suburban Foundations of the New Congress"

25   Masotti, Louis H., and Hadden, Jeffrey K., eds. SUBURBIA IN TRANSITION. New York: New Viewpoints, 1974.

Masotti and Hadden have put together a carefully selected collection of articles from the NEW YORK TIMES on suburbia. Most of the items included first appeared in the 1960s or early 1970s and thus remain highly relevant descriptions of suburban life and problems today. Among the topics are the suburban myth, the suburbs and race relations, the dispersal of commerce and industry, the politics of exclusion, crime and other suburban problems, the politics of suburbia, and past and future suburban development. Although a number of articles focus on the suburbs around New York, others pinpoint Black Jack, Missouri; Warren, Michigan; Dayton, Ohio; and other areas.

26   _____. THE URBANIZATION OF THE SUBURBS. Urban Affairs Annual Reviews, vol. 7. Beverly Hills, Calif.: Sage Publications, 1973.

From 1973 to 1976 five major collections of original articles on suburbia were published. In many ways, these contain the best of contemporary scholarship on American suburbia and most fully reflect where suburban study is today. They also illustrate the most purely suburban (suburbs qua suburbs) research.

The first of these was THE URBANIZATION OF THE SUBURBS. While not systematically structured to reflect a single point of view or theoretical perspective, the most common theme of these articles is the gradual evolution of suburbia into one integrated urban whole with the central city. Thus, for the urbanized suburbia, political boundaries are the most significant, and perhaps the only difference between the suburbs and the central city. Where differences appear, they are related to population characteristics and a suburb's development stage rather than geographical location or some inherent special attributes of the suburban environment.

The essays included in THE URBANIZATION OF THE SUBURBS run across a wide range. Only a few topics--education, crime, mental health, personal behavior, religion, and the arts--are conspicuously absent. The list of the contributions in addition to the lengthy preface follows:

Singleton, Gregory H. "The Genesis of Suburbia:
A Complex of Historical Trends"

Hadden, Jeffrey K., and Barton, Josef J. "An
Image that Will Not Die: Thoughts on the History of Anti-Urban Ideology"

Glenn, Norval D. "Suburbanization in the United
States since World War II"

Marshall, Harvey. "Suburban Life Styles: A Contribution to the Debate"

Greer, Scott. "The Family in Suburbia"

Pendleton, William W. "Blacks in Suburbs"

Hahn, Harlan. "Ethnic Minorities: Politics and
the Family in Suburbia"

Scott, Thomas M. "Suburban Governmental Structures"

Friesema, H. Paul. "Cities, Suburbs, and Short-
lived Models of Metropolitan Politics"

Zikmund, Joseph II. "Suburbs in State and National Politics"

Downes, Brian T. "Problem-solving in Suburbia:
The Basis for Political Conflict"

Babcock, Richard F. "Exclusionary Zoning: A
Code Phrase for a Notable Legal Struggle"

Rubinowitz, Leonard S. "A Question of Choice:
Access of the Poor and the Black to Suburban
Housing."

Ostrom, Elinor, and Parks, Roger B. "Suburban
Police Departments: Too Many and Too Small"

Thompson, Wilbur R. "A Preface to Suburban
Economics"

Berry, Brian J.L., and Cohen, Yehoshua S. "Decentralization of Commerce and Industry: The
Restructuring of Metropolitan America"

Wirt, Frederick M. "Financial and Desegregation
Reform in Suburbia"

Weissbourd, Bernard. "The Satellite Community as
Suburb"

Masotti, Louis H. "Epilogue: Suburbia in the
Seventies . . . and Beyond"

In sum, a good collection which accurately reflected the state
of suburban research in the early 1970s. Extensive bibliography.

27   Schnore, Leo F. THE URBAN SCENE. New York: Free Press, 1965.

An extraordinary collection of essays previously published by
Schnore from 1957 to 1965. Most either focus directly on
suburbia or touch on suburban topics.

28   Schwartz, Barry, ed. THE CHANGING FACE OF THE SUBURBS. Chicago:
      University of Chicago Press, 1976.

      This collection of original essays on suburbia may be one of
      the most carefully integrated readers ever created. In the
      preface Schwartz describes a process in which ten of the thir-
      teen contributors were assigned topics and then brought to-
      gether a year later to hear each others' papers and to evolve
      a collective perspective.

      There can be no question that several of the individual selec-
      tions make important and unique contributions to the literature
      on suburbia. Of these, Schwartz's own piece in which he
      seriously challenges the "urbanization of the suburbs" thesis
      is particularly interesting. The list of contents follows:

           Farley, Reynolds. "Components of Suburban Popu-
              lation Growth"
           Long, Larry H., and Glick, Paul. "Family Pat-
              terns in Suburban Areas: Recent Trends"
           Schnore, Leo F., André, Carolyn D., and Sharp,
              Harry. "Black Suburbanization, 1930-1970"
           Tobin, Gary. "Suburbanization and the Develop-
              ment of Motor Transportation Technology and the
              Suburbanization Process"
           Kasarda, John D. "The Changing Occupational
              Structure of the American Metropolis: Apropos
              the Urban Problem"
           Guterbock, Thomas M. "The Push Hypothesis:
              Minority Presence, Crime, and Urban Deconcen-
              tration"
           Zimmer, Basil G. "Suburbanization and Changing
              Political Structures"
           Greer, Ann Lennarson, and Greer, Scott. "Sub-
              urban Political Behavior: A Matter of Trust"
           Berry, Brian J.L., et al. "Attitudes toward In-
              tegration: The Role of Status in Community Re-
              sponse to Racial Change"
           Newman, William M. "Religion in Suburban
              America"
           Fischer, Claude S., and Jackson, Robert Max.
              "Suburbs, Networks, and Attitudes"
           Donaldson, Scott A. "The Machines in Cheever's
              Garden"
           Schwartz, Barry. "Images of Suburbia: Some Re-
              visionist Commentary and Conclusions"

29   "The Suburbs: Frontier of the 70's." CITY 5 (January-February 1971):
      entire issue.

      In-depth discussions of patterns in eleven major metropolitan
      areas (New York, Los Angeles, Denver, Indianapolis, Min-

neapolis-St. Paul, Baltimore, Atlanta, Chicago, Philadelphia, Cleveland, and Washington) are provided. Other articles discuss minority views of suburbia; black arts in Reston, Virginia; Warren, Michigan's rejection of HUD funds; and voter conflicts in the San Fernando Valley, among others.

30   URBAN AFFAIRS QUARTERLY   4 (June 1969): 421-519.

This issue of URBAN AFFAIRS QUARTERLY was devoted exclusively to suburban patterns and issues. All of the selections are original and several made seminal contributions to the study of American suburbia. The issue contents follow:

> Schnore, Leo F., and Jones, Joy K.O. "The Evolution of City-Suburban Types in the Course of a Decade"
> Zikmund, Joseph II, and Smith, Robert. "Political Participation in an Upper-Middle-Class Suburb"
> Hamovitch, William, and Levenson, Albert [M.]. "Projecting Suburban Employment"
> Downes, Brian T. "Issue Conflict, Factionalism, and Concensus in Suburban City Councils"
> Pinkerton, James R. "City-Suburban Residential Patterns by Social Class: A Review of the Literature"

31   Zschock, Dieter K., ed. ECONOMIC ASPECTS OF SUBURBAN GROWTH. Stony Brook, N.Y.: Economic Research Bureau of the State University of New York at Stony Brook, 1969.

A collection of essays on suburban development in Nassau and Suffolk Counties, New York (Long Island). All of the contributions are original to this collection:

> Hoover, Edgar M. "Introduction: Suburban Growth and Regional Analyses"
> Tobier, Emanuel. "Suburban Growth in the Metropolitan Setting"
> Hamovitch, William. "Trends and Objectives in Suburban Development"
> Zschock, Dieter K. "Poverty Amid Affluence in Suburbia"
> Netzer, Dick. "Financing Suburban Development"
> Levenson, Albert M. "Problems of Regional Analysis"

In addition there are two commentary pieces by Lee K. Koppleman and Robert Lekachman.

D. METROPOLITAN ATLAS SERIES

32 Abler, Ronald, and Adams, John S. A COMPARATIVE ATLAS OF AMERICA'S
    GREAT CITIES: TWENTY METROPOLITAN REGIONS. Minneapolis: Asso-
    ciation of American Geographers and University of Minnesota Press, 1976.

> In many ways the subtitle is more accurate than the title, for
> the scale of maps and the comparative data make city-to-city
> work difficult and intracity analysis virtually impossible. In-
> formation on housing, population demography, ethnicity, occu-
> pations, travel to work, and schools is presented.

> Also in this series: John S. Adams, ed. URBAN POLICY-
> MAKING AND METROPOLITAN DYNAMICS. Cambridge,
> Mass.: Ballinger, 1976.

33 Adams, John S., ed. CONTEMPORARY METROPOLITAN AMERICA.
    4 vols. Cambridge, Mass.: Ballinger, 1976.

> These volumes from the Comparative Metropolitan Analysis
> Project sponsored by the Association of American Geographers
> provide concise sketches of metropolitan development in twenty
> areas. Published in four volumes, the first treats Boston, New
> York, Philadelphia, and central Connecticut. The second,
> subtitled "Nineteenth Century Ports," covers Baltimore, New
> Orleans, and San Francisco Bay. The third looks at Pitts-
> burgh, St. Louis, Cleveland, Chicago, Detroit, Minneapolis-
> St. Paul, and Seattle. In the final volume are the twentieth-
> century cities--Dallas-Forth Worth, Miami, Houston, Atlanta,
> Los Angeles, and Washington. Each case study covers sub-
> urban as well as central city history, development, and con-
> temporary patterns.

> These four volumes provide extremely useful information for
> students and researchers. A number of the individual area
> sketches have been published separately in paperback for
> classroom purposes.

II. METROPOLITAN GROWTH AND DEVELOPMENT

A. SUBURBANIZATION DEVELOPMENT PROCESS

34 Anton, Thomas J. "Three Models of Community Development in the U.S."
    PUBLIUS 1 (Winter 1972): 11-37.

> Examines three models of community development to determine
> how suburbs develop, which actors become involved, and how
> and why they do. Anton describes the social choice process
> of Lincolnwood, Illinois, from 1829 to 1925; the mixed bar-
> gaining system of Lincolnwood from 1925 to 1960; and the ad-
> ministered choice system of Levittown, New Jersey. The au-
> thor concludes that there is a powerful trend toward greater
> involvement by public agencies, greater use of public planning
> criteria, fewer but more bureaucratized actors, and increase
> in the size, scope, and resources of projects.

35 Birch, David L. "From Suburb to Urban Place." ANNALS OF THE
    AMERICAN ACADEMY OF POLITICAL AND SOCIAL SCIENCE 422
    (1975): 25-35.

> Birch predicts that the process of suburbanization will even-
> tually transform the suburbs into self-generating urban places
> in their own right. It is likely that they will form a hier-
> archy, with each suburb being a node on an interdependent
> network. Implications of this prediction are discussed.

36 Brown, David L. "The Redistribution of Physicians and Dentists in Incor-
    porated Places of the Upper Midwest, 1950-1970." RURAL SOCIOLOGY
    39 (Summer 1974): 205-23.

> Analysis and comparison of the spatial distribution of six cate-
> gories of medical professionals over a twenty-year period.
> Brown found that most medical categories, especially general
> practitioners and specialists in primary care, were less cen-
> tralized in 1970 than 1950. Physicians and dentists were the
> most suburbanized of the six categories.

37   Burns, Elizabeth K. "The Process of Suburban Residential Development:
      The San Francisco Peninsula." GREAT PLAINS-ROCKY MOUNTAIN
      GEOGRAPHICAL JOURNAL 3 (1974): 10-17.

      Theoretical discussion of the stages of suburbanization as linked
      to the primary modes of transportation at different times. San
      Francisco peninsula is used as an example to illustrate the theory.

38   Dluhy, Milan J. "The Dynamics of Suburban Community Development."
      In STRATEGIES OF COMMUNITY ORGANIZATION, 2d ed., edited by
      Fred M. Cox et al., pp. 117-27. Itasca, Ill.: F.E. Peacock Publishers,
      1974.

      Author is concerned with factors which influence a suburb's
      exercise of control over growth and development within its
      own boundaries. Data from eight Detroit suburbs suggest lead-
      ership continuity and support for planning as the most important
      variables. Other community characteristics also were tested
      and found to have an influence. Finally, level of community
      control was directly related to the outside image of the com-
      munity within the metropolitan area.

39   Edel, Matthew. "The Distribution of Real Estate Value Changes: Metro-
      politan Boston, 1870-1970." JOURNAL OF URBAN ECONOMICS 2
      (October 1975): 366-87.

      Analyzes the pattern of real estate change among seventy-eight
      Boston suburbs from 1870 to 1970 and concludes that within
      developed areas the lowest increments in land and house values
      occurred closer to the central business district of Boston. The
      net effect is to redistribute wealth regressively among home
      owners.

40   Edmonston, Berry, and Davis, Omar. "Population Suburbanization in the
      Western Region of the United States, 1900-1970." LAND ECONOMICS
      52 (August 1976): 393-403.

      A general study of suburbanization patterns in metropolitan
      areas west of the Great Plains. Analysis based on changing
      density gradient from 1900 to 1970.

41   French, Robert M., and Hadden, Jeffrey K. "Mobile Homes: Instant
      Suburbia or Transportable Slums?" SOCIAL PROBLEMS 16 (Fall 1968):
      219-26.

      Authors present available evidence to dispute the contention that mobile
      home parks in the suburbs are a means of escape from the inner city for
      young middle-class families who cannot afford a suburban home. Instead,
      the majority of suburban mobile home residents are blue-collar workers
      who are recent immigrants from rural areas, attracted by the easy financing
      and complete furnishing of a mobile home.

42   Gallaway, Lowell E. "Urban Decay and the Labor Market." QUAR-
      TERLY REVIEW OF ECONOMICS AND BUSINESS 7 (Winter 1967): 7-16.

      Description of a dynamic process by which the tendency for
      individuals to move to the suburbs becomes progressively stronger,
      accelerating the process of adverse population selection and
      human decay in central cities. The hypothesis is tested with
      a case study of southern Los Angeles suburbs. The author is
      particularly interested in assessing the influence of the labor
      market on individuals' residential location decisions.

43   Goldfield, David R. "The Limits of Suburban Growth: The Washington,
      D.C. SMSA." URBAN AFFAIRS QUARTERLY 12 (September 1976): 83-
      102.

      Zikmund, Joseph II. "The Limits of Suburban Growth: A Comment."
      URBAN AFFAIRS QUARTERLY 12 (September 1976): 103-6.

      Hadden, Jeffrey K. "The Limits of Suburban Growth: A Comment."
      URBAN AFFAIRS QUARTERLY 12 (September 1976): 107-11.

      Goldfield, David R. "A Reply to Professors Zikmund and Hadden."
      URBAN AFFAIRS QUARTERLY 12 (September 1976): 112-16.

      Goldfield attempts to predict the limits of suburban growth
      with a case study of the Washington, D.C. metropolitan area
      which analyzes four related growth factors--fertility and family
      formation trends, housing, transportation, and central city re-
      habilitation. In their comments, Zikmund and Hadden cast
      doubt on the strength and direction of the trends as interpreted
      by Goldfield and caution against generalizing the experience
      of the Washington area to the national scene. Goldfield re-
      sponds that Washington's atypicality makes it a prototype of a
      new national trend in the revitalization of central cities and
      retrenchment of suburban areas.

44   Harvey, Robert O., and Clark, W.A.V. "The Nature and Economics of
      Urban Sprawl." LAND ECONOMICS 41 (February 1965): 1-9.

      A general "think piece" on the topic of suburbanization and
      urban sprawl. Among the topics briefly addressed are the
      physical pattern, causes, and costs of sprawl.

45   Hills, Stuart L. "The Planned Suburban Community." LAND ECONOMICS
      45 (May 1969): 277-82.

      Exploration of the unanticipated consequences of living in an os-
      tensibly planning community. In this case study of an unnamed
      blue-collar suburb, the builders employed many misleading and
      deceptive inducements to suburban living but did not plan for fu-
      ture growth or provide housing for a balanced community of all
      ages, lifestyles, and income levels.

46   Hoover, Edgar M., and Vernon, Raymond. ANATOMY OF A METROPOLIS.
      New York: Regional Plan Association, 1959.

      One of the first--and still one of the very best--attempts to
      provide a total social and economic picture of a major metro-
      politan area in geographic perspective. Based largely on data
      from the 1950 census, the book remains only marginally useful
      as a description of the New York region today. By contrast,
      the general patterns and trends described are still operative
      both in and around New York City and other metropolitan
      areas. The book is important now as a model of a good met-
      ropolitan study and as a theoretical discussion of metropolitan
      development generally.

      After delineating the areas of study and the primary subregions
      within, the authors focus on economic activity as a major de-
      terminant of regional growth and metropolitan geography. Chang-
      ing spatial needs of various economic activities influence lo-
      cational decisions which in turn affect the geographic distri-
      bution of jobs, local tax bases, and the locational needs of
      other economic activities. In turn, people tend to live where
      they have satisfactory access to jobs, and commercial estab-
      lishments follow their customers.

      ANATOMY OF A METROPOLIS is more than a classic; it is
      today absolutely basic.

47   Jackson, Kenneth T. "The Crabgrass Frontier: 150 Years of Suburban
      Growth in America." In THE URBAN EXPERIENCE, edited by Raymond
      A. Mohl and James F. Richardson, pp. 196-211. Belmont, Calif.: Wads-
      worth Publishing Co., 1973.

      Good historical treatment of suburbanization in America. Dis-
      cusses general patterns in three historical eras: pre-1910, pre-
      World War II, and post-World War II.

48   _____. "Urban Deconcentration in the Nineteenth Century." In THE
      NEW URBAN HISTORY, edited by Leo F. Schnore, pp. 110-42. Prince-
      ton, N.J.: Princeton University Press, 1975.

      Jackson explores the concept of "urban deconcentration" pri-
      marily through an analysis of patterns in Philadelphia during
      the nineteenth century. Five definitions of deconcentration
      are proposed and illustrated historically: (1) proportion of
      people living outside the central city, (2) lowering of area-
      wide population densities, (3) decline in core population,
      (4) outward movement of higher socioeconomic status level
      urban residents, and (5) increasing residence-work distances.
      The author concludes that urban deconcentration, if not sub-
      urbanization, is certainly an urban phenomenon with long his-
      torical roots.

49   Kasarda, John D., and Redfearn, George V. "Differential Patterns of City and Suburban Growth in the United States." JOURNAL OF URBAN HISTORY 2 (November 1975): 43-66.

> Study of metropolitan population growth and distribution as influenced by central city annexation of surrounding suburban areas. Primary data used were census results from 1900 to 1970. Findings related both to the development of central cities and to the patterns of suburbanization around those cities.

50   McKee, David L., and Smith, Gerald H. "Environmental Diseconomies in Suburban Expansion." AMERICAN JOURNAL OF ECONOMICS AND SOCIOLOGY 31 (April 1972): 181-88.

> A general overview which attributes sprawl to actions in the marketplace and suggests the need for greater cooperation among local governments and planning agencies.

51   Mark, Harold, and Schwirian, Kent P. "Ecological Position, Urban Central Place Function and Community Population Growth." AMERICAN JOURNAL OF SOCIOLOGY 73 (July 1967): 30-41.

> Examination using census data of the general relationship between urban central place function and community population growth as a function of both the level of regional industrialization and of the particular ecological position of the suburb in the total pattern of intrametropolitan relations. Authors conclude that central place function is no longer a significant community-building activity. Rather, population growth is due to other expansions of the local economic base, and different growth factors operate for different classes of cities. Suburbs' growth is due to their proximity to metropolitan centers and their roles as dormitories or industrial satellites.

52   Neutze, Max. THE SUBURBAN APARTMENT BOOM. Washington, D.C.: Resources for the Future, 1968.

> In the first two decades after World War II suburban development consisted primarily of single-family homes. Apartments were assumed to represent a lower quality of development and in many communities were openly discouraged if not prohibited. Yet the introduction of multifamily housing into suburbia was virtually inevitable--at first on a small scale, later as a major form of new housing construction.
>
> Neutze describes the emergence of this new pattern across the nation and then provides a detailed analysis of apartment construction in the Washington, D.C. metropolitan area during the early 1960s. Most useful are his comments on the causes of the new apartment boom and his descriptions of the factors affecting the location of apartments in suburban situations.

53   Peters, Terry Spielman. THE POLITICS AND ADMINISTRATION OF
     LAND USE CONTROL. Lexington, Mass.: Lexington Books, 1974.

     Case study of land use and development control in a suburban
     county.   Immediately to the west of the District of Columbia
     in Virginia, Fairfax County had been deluged for twenty years
     with massive suburbanization.   In June 1973, the County Board
     of Supervisors adopted a Planning and Land Use System (PLUS)
     intended to limit and control further development.   Peter's
     study describes the conditions which led to the creation and
     operation of PLUS.   Legitimation of the new scheme, policy
     making within its guiding structure, program development, and
     implementation all come under careful scrutiny.

     For an update on PLUS see Thomas Grubisich, "Fairfax Votes
     No on PLUS." PLANNING 40 (March–April 1976): 44–46.

54   Rabinovitz, Francine F., and Lamore, James. "After Suburbia, What?
     --- The New Communities Movement in Los Angeles." In LOS ANGELES,
     edited by Werner Z. Hersch, pp. 169–206. New York: Praeger, 1971.

     Authors argue that traditional suburban patterns no longer guar-
     antee values sought by middle Americans. The "new com-
     munity" movement is suggested as the next step in the search
     for peace and security. Westlake residents come from existing
     suburban areas and emphasize social homogeneity and the pos-
     itive physical and environmental aspects of the community in
     explaining their moves. Authors conclude with misgivings that
     on the separate issues of environment versus the central city
     the middle class is beginning to make the former their primary
     concern.

55   Real Estate Research Corporation. THE COSTS OF SPRAWL. 3 vols.
     Washington, D.C.: Government Printing Office, 1975.

     These three volumes contain the most thorough theoretical analysis
     of the costs of low-density residential construction published
     to date. Cost estimates are generated and compared for six
     hypothetical communities: high-density planned, low-density
     planned, and unplanned (sprawl), plus three medium-density.
     Each community is tested on the basis of four factors: energy
     consumption, environmental impact, capital cost, and operating
     cost. The most significant findings are those contrasting the
     high-density planned case versus the low-density unplanned.
     Sprawl was judged to be clearly the least desirable in relation
     to all four factors. While the conclusions of the study are
     subject to criticism, on the whole it represents an important
     breakthrough in the study of suburban sprawl and community
     planning generally.

     See also Alan Altsluter's review of this study in the JOURNAL
     OF THE AMERICAN INSTITUTE OF PLANNERS 63 (April 1977):
     207–9.

56   Rivkin, Malcolm D. "Growth Control via Sewer Moratoria." URBAN
      LAND 33 (March 1974): 10-15.

      General discussion of use of sewer moratoria in the United
      States to limit urban-suburban growth. Data presented on a
      national and state basis.

57   Sinclair, Robert; Shipton, Robert; and Willis, Helen. "A Case Study of
      Urban Expansion in Southwestern Macomb County, Michigan." MICHIGAN
      ACADEMICIAN 4 (Fall 1971): 161-81.

      This is a case study of land-use changes in a three-mile strip
      north of Detroit from 1948 to 1968. The authors propose a
      six-step process of land conversion from rural to suburban ac-
      tivity. Maps comparing the two time periods provide clear
      illustrations of the processes described.

58   Stonier, Charles E. "Planning in the Maturing Suburb." TRAFFIC QUAR-
      TERLY 19 (April 1965): 285-95.

      After reviewing the major demographic, commutation, tax, and
      governmental issues which planners in older suburbs must con-
      sider in providing public transportation, Stonier describes sev-
      eral obstacles to effective planning: fragmentation of govern-
      mental responsibility, difficulty in obtaining funding from state
      legislatures, citizen reaction, and federal funding restrictions.
      The author concludes that a cohesive urban transportation policy
      entails the cooperation of all agencies concerned with trans-
      portation, the development of a system to incorporate all modes
      of transportation, a major effort by governments to educate the
      public, and regional planning.

59   Stuart, Darwin G., and Teska, Robert B. "Who Pays for What: A Cost
      Revenue Analysis of Suburban Land Use Alternatives." URBAN LAND
      30 (March 1971): 3-16.

      Outlines a basic work for a cost-revenue analysis of the im-
      pact of a suburban residential development on the provision
      of public services. Use is illustrated with a case study of
      school services in Barrington, Illinois.

60   Warner, Sam Bass, Jr. STREETCAR SUBURBS: THE PROCESS OF GROWTH
      IN BOSTON 1870-1900. Cambridge, Mass.: Harvard University Press
      and M.I.T. Press, 1962.

      STREETCAR SUBURBS is one of a small number of historical
      case studies of urbanization and suburbanization before the
      turn of the century. Using three communities to illustrate
      general urban growth patterns, Warner provides concrete ex-
      amples of the geographers' and urban economists' theories.

The author links Boston's development to the stages of transportation technology dominant at the time that area was set-
tled. Thus, Warner finds a core pedestrian city, the streetcar
suburbs of the last quarter of the nineteenth century, and the
newer suburbs which emerged after 1900. In addition, even
the earliest suburbs were differentiated on the basis of the
social class composition of their residents.

STREETCAR SUBURBS now must be viewed as a historical classic.
It is still good history, and an important contribution to our
contemporary understanding of suburbia.

See also Allen M. Wakstein, "Boston's Search for a Metropolitan Solution." JOURNAL OF THE AMERICAN INSTITUTE
OF PLANNERS 38 (September 1972): 285-96.

61   Wheaton, William L.C. "Public and Private Agents of Change in Urban
      Expansion." In EXPLORATIONS INTO URBAN STRUCTURE, edited by
      Melvin M. Webber, pp. 154-96. Philadelphia: University of Pennsyl-
      vania Press, 1964.

      Early exploration of the role of private and public investment
      decisions in affecting urban development. Author emphasizes
      the tremendously large number of decisions which aggregate
      to create metropolitan growth trends. Other important factors
      include market forces, the size and character of investors, in-
      terdependence within the investment process, professional stan-
      dards, bureaucratic procedures, and public policies.

62   Williams, Barbara R. "St. Louis: A City and Its Suburbs." FOCUS/
      MIDWEST 9, no. 61 (1974): 20-47.

      Descriptive article on metropolitan development in and around
      St. Louis.

B. RURAL-URBAN LAND CONVERSION

63   Archer, R.W. "Land Speculation and Scattered Development; Failures in
      the Urban-Fringe Land Market." URBAN STUDIES 10 (October 1973):
      367-72.

      Case study of development on the fringe of Lexington, Ken-
      tucky. In particular, the author explores the phenomenon of
      developmental leapfroging--subdividing land out beyond the
      boundaries of continuous urbanization. Landholder and home
      buyer behavior is critically analyzed. Imperfections in the
      market system are highlighted and suggestions for modification
      are proposed.

64   Birch, David L.   "Toward a Stage Theory of Urban Growth." JOURNAL
      OF THE AMERICAN INSTITUTE OF PLANNERS 37 (March 1971): 78-87.

      Theoretical analysis of the pattern of urban development. The
      author argues that urbanization passes through six distinct stages
      from rural land use to urban recapture (renewal). Data from
      the New Haven area are used to illustrate the theory.

65   Blase, Melvin G., and Staub, William J.   "Real Property Taxes in the
      Rural-Urban Fringe." LAND ECONOMICS 47 (May 1971): 168-74.

      Authors surveyed 153 farmers in one urban, three suburban,
      and three rural counties around Kansas City, Missouri, in order
      to determine the degree to which urbanization affects property
      taxes and to test the statistical significance of sixteen socio-
      economic variables hypothesized to be related to the amount
      of real property tax paid per acre. Findings indicate that in
      general farmers did not lose their ability to pay taxes over
      the four years studied. Farmers in the urban county did pay
      more tax per acre and were less able to pay out of current
      budgets, but their land appreciated more than in the other
      six counties.

66   Clawson, Marion. SUBURBAN LAND CONVERSION IN THE UNITED
      STATES. Baltimore: Johns Hopkins Press, 1971.

      This is the most definitive treatment of how land passes from
      rural to suburban usage. The book is divided into two roughly
      equal parts. The first is a general discussion of the land con-
      version process. The second looks specifically at the north-
      eastern urban complex and at the Washington, D.C., Wilmington,
      Delaware, and Springfield, Massachusetts, SMSAs in particular.
      In effect, the book serves as a chronological continuation to
      Jean Gottmann's MEGALOPOLIS (New York: Twentieth Cen-
      tury Fund, 1961) and Hoover and Vernon's ANATOMY OF A
      METROPOLIS (see item 46) and as a major original contribu-
      tion to the suburban literature.

      Clawson seeks to present a comprehensive view of the large
      and complex subject of land use changes at the suburban
      fringe. After several introductory chapters on urbanization
      in the United States since the end of World War II, the au-
      thor examines in depth the decision-making process in urban
      expansion. A number of basic actors in the process are iden-
      tified and their roles elaborated: home buyers, home builders,
      planners, local governmental officials, lenders, landowners,
      land speculators, and real estate agents, among others. Other
      topics considered include the housing market, public services,
      and the externality implications of the present market system.

      Clawson concludes that the land conversion process is highly
      dispersed and fragmented, with actors working in conflict as

well as cooperation with each other. Consequences of this process are a great deal of vacant or unused land within the urbanized area at any particular time, rapidly rising prices for suburban land, and the passing of externality costs from developers and new home owners to established residents and older areas in the metropolitan region. Clawson sees both advantages and disadvantages to the present system and recommends significant changes to improve the workings of this fundamental process.

This book is one of the most important suburban studies in the last ten years and is destined to be a classic.

67   Graf, William L. "Streams, Slopes, and Suburban Development." GEO-GRAPHICAL ANALYSIS 8 (April 1976): 157-73.

Discusses the impact of suburbanization on water systems and other geological features around Denver.

68   Hansen, David E., and Schwartz, S.I. "Landowner Behavior at the Rural-Urban Fringe in Response to Preferential Property Taxation." LAND ECONOMICS 51 (November 1975): 341-54.

Study of the impact of the California Land Conservation Act (1965) on fringe development in the Sacramento area. Findings suggest the greater the likelihood of development, the less likely the owner will participate in CLCA preferential tax schemes. Primary benefit of the program appears to be for farmers who desire to continue farming.

69   Hills, Stuart L. "Siege of a Village." NATIONAL CIVIC REVIEW 56 (February 1967): 75-80.

This case study of the suburbanization of an unidentified village on the outskirts of a large metropolis describes the sudden and dramatic changes wrought by the building of an adjacent large residential development. Hill sketches the conflict which arises between the old and new residents over politics, retailing, government organization, education, and religion.

70   Hushak, Leroy J. "The Urban Demand for Urban-Fringe Land." URBAN ECONOMICS 51 (May 1975): 112-23.

Vrooman, David H. "The Urban Demand for Urban-Rural Fringe Land: A Comment." LAND ECONOMICS 53 (February 1977): 130.

Hushak, Leroy J. "The Urban Demand for Urban-Rural Fringe Land: A Reply." LAND ECONOMICS 53 (February 1977): 131-32.

Hushak's objective is to estimate and analyze an urban demand function for underdeveloped (agricultural) land in the urban-rural fringe with the use of actual land transactions in Franklin County (Columbus), Ohio. Results show that lot size and type of zoning affect demand for public services, property values, and tax revenue, but that the impact of property taxes on land prices is small. In his comment, Vrooman points out that Hushak's equations are faulty because they fail to account for the supply function, which Vrooman defines as the amount of land offered for sale under various conditions. Hushak responds by discussing the problems of applying traditional concepts to the land market and attempting to clarify his conceptual assumptions.

71   Kaiser, Edward J., and Weiss, Shirley F. "Public Policy and the Residential Development Process." JOURNAL OF THE AMERICAN INSTITUTE OF PLANNERS 34 (January 1970): 30-37.

Theoretical discussion of the land conversion process from rural to urban (suburban) uses.

72   Kaiser, Edward J., et al. "Predicting the Behavior of Predevelopment Landowners on the Urban Fringe." JOURNAL OF THE AMERICAN INSTITUTE OF PLANNERS 34 (September 1968): 328-33.

Development of a theory to predict how rural or nonurban landowners will respond to urbanization pressures. Model tested with positive results on two North Carolina metropolitan areas.

73   Pryor, Robin J. "Defining the Rural-Urban Fringe." SOCIAL FORCES 47 (December 1968): 202-15.

Reviews sixty case studies of rural-urban fringe areas with the goal of summarizing the characteristics of the fringe and integrating the structural and functional aspects of the fringe with theories of urban invasion. Particularly valuable for the extensive international bibliography of work done in the 1950s on this topic.

74   Schmid, A. Allan. CONVERTING LAND FROM RURAL TO URBAN USES. Washington, D.C.: Resources for the Future, 1968.

This study looks at the conversion of rural land to urban purposes from an economic perspective. First, Schmid examines how land values appreciate as development becomes imminent. Next, he describes the costs of this conversion process. The author emphasized the seller's dominance in this land market and suggests that the consumer's power to dictate the character of the "suburban product" is highly overstated. Greater consumer sovereignty and a wider range of options are proposed to correct the market imbalance identified.

A shorter version of this material can be found in A. Allan Schmid, "Suburban Land Appreciation and Public Policy." JOURNAL OF THE AMERICAN INSTITUTE OF PLANNERS 36 (January 1970): 38-43.

75   Strong, Ann L.   "Factors Affecting Land Tenure in the Urban Fringe." URBAN LAND 25 (November 1966): 1,3-6.

Summary of Strong's book, OPEN SPACE FOR URBAN AMERICA (Urban Renewal Administration, 1965). Strong surveyed owners of land parcels of at least five acres in eight townships in Pennsylvania in order to determine their reasons for selling or retaining land. Sales prices were found to be related to the location and size of individual parcels and the purchaser's planned use, not the seller's motivations. The majority of purchasers did not plan to increase population density or land use intensity so that open space was not immediately threatened.

76   Wolfe, M.R.   "A Chronology of Land Tenure." TOWN PLANNING RE-VIEW   37 (January 1967): 271-90.

A geographical case study of the suburbanization process around Seattle. Article concentrates on the role of large landholders in the transition from rural to suburban land uses.

77   Wyckoff, J.C. "Impact of Suburbanization on Rural Towns." JOURNAL OF THE COMMUNITY DEVELOPMENT SOCIETY 4 (Spring 1973): 48-57.

Case study of the suburbanization process in the Springfield-Chicopee-Holyoke, Massachusetts, SMSA. Shows that rural land was being converted to urban uses at a very rapidly ac-celerating rate despite the relatively slow population increase. Wyckoff finds that the existing mechanisms for controlling growth--planning, zoning, and intergovernmental aid--were not always used, and he discusses the policy implications of the loss of agricultural land and the various alternatives avail-able for influencing the suburbanization process.

C. ANNEXATION

78   Bromley, David G., and Smith, Joel.   "The Historical Significance of Annexation as a Social Process." LAND ECONOMICS 49 (August 1973): 294-309.

Expands previous analyses of annexation to more cities and systematizes available information in order to examine the ex-tent of annexation and the distribution of annexation activity over time. Authors find some common patterns, such as the

tendencies for the frequency of annexation to decline with
city age, the largest single increase to come after 50,000
population is reached, and the activity to fluctuate indepen-
dently of the restrictiveness of state annexation statutes. They
conclude that annexation has been significant to the growth
of all the cities studied but that the individual growth experiences have been extremely varied.

79   Jackson, Kenneth T. "Metropolitan Government versus Suburban Autonomy."
In CITIES IN AMERICAN HISTORY, edited by Kenneth T. Jackson and
Stanley K. Schultz, pp. 442-62. New York: Knopf, 1972.

The author seeks to test Kingsley Davis's assertion that annexation is not a major factor to be studied in urban geography.
By looking at city area and population growth and loss patterns in forty major American cities from 1850 to 1970, the
author shows the direct relationship between population growth
and areal growth. Finally, Jackson discusses why annexation
by central cities in some areas stopped or significantly slowed
after 1910.

80   Manis, Jerome G. "Urbanism and Annexation Attitudes in Two Similar
Suburban Areas." AMERICAN JOURNAL OF ECONOMICS AND SO-
CIOLOGY 27 (October 1968): 347-63.

Report of survey data from 545 suburban residents in two communities outside Kalamazoo, Michigan. Despite similarities
in the communities, their past experiences with annexations
were quite different. Neither personal backgrounds nor political attitudes adequately explained differences in views toward
annexation. Author suggests political leadership may have significant impact in this area.

81   Mushkatel, Alvin H.; Wilson, L.A. II; and Mushkatel, Linda G. "A
Model of Citizen Response to Annexation." URBAN AFFAIRS QUARTERLY
9 (December 1973): 139-63.

After carefully reviewing the literature on central city annexations, the authors develop a model of citizen response to such
annexations. A case study of an annexation attempt by Port-
land, Oregon, is presented.

82   Schnidman, Frank. "Annexation Agreements." URBAN LAND 35 (June
1976): 7-16.

Discussion of annexation patterns in the United States. Special
attention is directed to Illinois, which recently led the nation
in municipal annexation. Though the suburban content is not
explicit, many of the examples are from the Chicago suburbs.

D. COMMERCE, INDUSTRY, TRANSPORTATION, AND COMMUNICATION

83 Armstrong, Regina Belz. THE OFFICE INDUSTRY. Cambridge, Mass.: M.I.T. Press, 1972.

This report from the Regional Plan Association of New York focuses on the growth of white-collar jobs in the metropolitan economy and the relation of office locations within the SMSA to the health and functioning of the regional economy. Considerable information is provided on central city versus suburban office location for metropolitan areas around the country. The patterns for the New York Consolidated Area are developed in detail. Final chapter explores options available to the New York region in its future planning, and considers the pluses and minuses of these options.

84 Cohen, Saul B., and Lewis, George K. "Form and Function in the Geography of Retailing." ECONOMIC GEOGRAPHY 43 (January 1967): 1-42.

Introduces a systematic approach to the analysis of form and function in the geography of retailing and applies it to the Boston and Detroit metropolitan areas. Authors stress the role of individual firms in creating spatial subsystems in the modern retailing configuration.

85 Drucker, Mark L. "Relocation to the Suburbs: Can Employees Find a New Home Too?" BUSINESS AND SOCIETY REVIEW/INNOVATION, no. 9, Spring 1974, pp. 40-46.

Citing many actual occurrences, author discusses the issues raised when a corporation relocating to a suburb decides to take an active role in making low-income housing available to its workers in the new location.

86 Fischel, William A. "Fiscal and Environmental Considerations in the Location of Firms in Suburban Communities." In FISCAL ZONING AND LAND USE CONTROLS, edited by Edwin S. Mills and Wallace E. Oates, pp. 119-73. Lexington, Mass.: D.C. Heath and Co., 1975.

Contends that the property tax provides the means of exchange between firms and residents of suburban communities. Residents voluntarily surrender some of their community environment by granting permission to firms to locate there in return for fiscal benefits from the firms. If the property tax system is an efficient exchange mechanism, then metropolitan zoning policies should deal only with intermunicipal spillovers. The author concludes that decentralized zoning and property taxation may not be as bad as is frequently asserted.

87   Fisher, Walter D., and Fisher, Marjorie C.L. "The Spatial Allocation of
      Employment and Residence in a Metropolitan Area." JOURNAL OF RE-
      GIONAL SCIENCE 15 (December 1975): 261-76.

      Authors estimate a small static intraurban model of six equa-
      tions to explain simultaneously the location of employment and
      residence in 100 neighborhoods and suburbs of Chicago.

88   Gannon, Colin A., and Dear, Michael J. "Rapid Transit and Office
      Development." TRAFFIC QUARTERLY 24 (April 1975): 223-42.

      Investigates the relationship between suburban commercial office
      development and the introduction of rail rapid transit facilities
      in order to confirm the hypothesis that a mass transit facility
      not only consolidates the central business district as a center
      for office location but also increases the attraction of nearby
      suburban locations and is a pivotal advantage for the develop-
      ment of viable suburban office locations.

89   Greytak, David. "Central City Access and the Journey to Work." SOCIO-
      ECONOMIC PLANNING SCIENCES 8 (February 1974): 57-58.

      In a methodological note, author attempts to evaluate empiri-
      cally the identification of metropolitan work trips with a jour-
      ney to the city center and considers the implications of con-
      tinued metropolitan decentralization for the relation between
      the two factors. Findings indicate that equating residential
      distance from the city center with the actual work trip dis-
      tance (as determined by a survey in northeastern New Jersey)
      significantly understates the latter and that the statistical
      validity of equating the two varies by the comparative rate of
      decentralization of work and residence places.

90   Guest, Avery M. "Journey to Work, 1960-1970." SOCIAL FORCES 54
      (September 1975): 220-25.

      A brief report on commuting and reverse commuting in ninety-
      eight SMSAs for 1960 and 1970.

91   _____. "Occupation and the Journey to Work." SOCIAL FORCES 55
      (September 1976): 166-81.

      A study of journey to work patterns across several metropolitan
      areas. Evidence suggests considerable intermetropolitan varia-
      tion, particularly in the patterns for high-status workers.

92   Guest, Avery M., and Cluett, Christopher. "Workplace and Residential
      Location: A Push-Pull Model." JOURNAL OF REGIONAL SCIENCE 16
      (December 1976): 399-410.

      Authors attempt to clarify the relationship between home and

workplace by testing a gravity model of intraurban residential
location which incorporates an analysis of three major factors
which "push" and "pull" workers toward particular suburbs--
housing quality, manufacturing concentration, and racial composition. Results suggest that commuting distances clearly con-
strain high-status workers and female workers, but not black
workers, and that for nonblack workers manufacturing activity
and a large black population are negative considerations. However, the authors conclude that the more complex push-pull
models are not appreciably better than simple gravity models
in explaining the relationship between home and workplace
within the suburban ring for most workers.

93   Hughes, James W., and James, Franklin J. "Changing Spatial Distributions
      of Jobs and Residences." GROWTH AND CHANGE 6 (July 1975): 20-25.

      Authors focus on the capacity of mass transit systems to adjust
      to changing patterns of work trips in New Jersey. These
      changes have been partially stimulated by freeway construction,
      and the problems of adjustment are further aggravated by re-
      strictive local zoning practices. They urge planners of mass
      transit facilities to consider long-distance commutation, cross-
      commutation, and reverse commutation as well as traditional
      suburb-to-central city commutation if their efforts are to be
      relevant to the work trips of the majority of workers.

94   Kain, John F. "The Distribution and Movement of Jobs and Industry."
      In THE METROPOLITAN ENIGMA, edited by James Q. Wilson, pp. 1-43.
      Garden City, N.Y.: Doubleday, Anchor Books, 1970.

      Author seeks to explore the motivation for, timing of, and im-
      pact of industrial dispersal in American metropolitan areas.
      This is a major study of job movement to the suburbs and a
      speculative analysis of the consequences of such patterns.

95   Logan, John R. "Industrialization and the Stratification of Cities in Sub-
      urban Regions." AMERICAN JOURNAL OF SOCIOLOGY 82 (September
      1976): 333-48.

      A significant analysis of the factors affecting the pattern of
      suburban growth in American metropolitan areas. The author
      suggests that a model for this process must include regional
      growth, suburban interdependence, local governmental decisions,
      social characteristics of residents, and the group politics within
      each community. Census data from 1950 to 1970 are used to
      generate tentative models.

96   Marando, Vincent L. "Metropolitanism, Transportation and Employment
      for the Central-City Poor." URBAN AFFAIRS QUARTERLY 10 (December
      1974): 158-69.

Marando presents data from the 1970 Census Employment Survey to reject the hypothesis that transportation factors act to keep unemployed residents of low-income city neighborhoods from available employment opportunities in the suburbs; examines alternative explanations for the suburban employment of low-income central city residents; and discusses some public policy implications of these problems. In general, author casts doubts on the feasibility of increasing expenditures on public transit and low-income housing in the suburbs in order to lower central-city unemployment.

97   Nunnally, Nelson, and Pollina, Ronald. "Recent Trends in Industrial Park Location in the Chicago Metropolitan Area." LAND ECONOMICS 49 (August 1973): 356-61.

Examination of post-World War II trends in the location of industrial parks in the Chicago metropolitan area and comparison of the locational attributes of the successful and unsuccessful parks.

98   Quante, Wolfgang. "The Suburban Experience." In his THE EXODUS OF CORPORATE HEADQUARTERS FROM NEW YORK CITY, pp. 108-16. New York: Praeger, 1976.

In these few pages the author presents a summary of opinions expressed by corporate executives in the New York area regarding corporate moves from the city to nearby suburbs. The attitudes expressed were generally positive toward the prospects or results of such a move.

99   Rachman, David J., and Levine, Marvin. "Blue Collar Workers Shape Suburban Market." JOURNAL OF RETAILING 42 (Winter 1966-67): 5-13.

Considers the impact and growth of blue-collar workers in the suburbs, the adjustments made by retailing institutions, and the implications for future marketing efforts. Authors cite the growth of discount apparel houses and bargain basement sections of major department stores to support their contention that the blue-collar suburbanite represents a distinct suburban market segment which needs different outlets and advertisements.

100   Simons, Peter L. "The Shape of Suburban Retail Market Areas: Implications from a Literature Review." JOURNAL OF RETAILING 49 (Winter 1973-74): 65-78.

Theoretical discussion of the difficulties encountered in specifying the shape of retail markets, particularly in suburban areas.

101 Tucker, Grady. "Site Selection for Suburban Shopping Centers." REAL ESTATE REVIEW 4 (Summer 1974): 70–76.

General description of the factors used by developers in the placement of suburban shopping centers. Emphasizes size, shape, physical characteristics, and costs of land plus the marketing potential of the surrounding area.

102 White, Michelle J. "Firm Suburbanization and Urban Subcenters." JOURNAL OF URBAN ECONOMICS 3 (October 1976): 323–43.

Presents a mathematical model of firm location in which jobs are located both at the urban center and at a suburban subcenter. White quantifies and discusses a firm's locational decision when both suburban and central business district export terminals exist, problems in ensuring an adequate labor supply in the suburbs, the effects of a firm's move on a suburb, and the public policy influences on a firm's suburban location decision.

103 Yu, Eui-Young. "Correlates of Commutation between Central Cities and Rings of SMSAs." SOCIAL FORCES 51 (September 1972): 74–86.

Author attempts to relate variations in metropolitan characteristics to variations in the rates of commutation between the central city and suburbs of ninety-five large SMSAs. Findings indicate that the level and direction of central city-suburban commutation in a particular SMSA is largely determined by its industrial and socioeconomic structure and the distribution of manufacturing jobs between city and suburbs.

III. SUBURBAN AND COMMUNITY CASE STUDIES

104   Berger, Bennett M. WORKING-CLASS SUBURB. Berkeley and Los Angeles: University of California Press, 1960.

One of the true classics of the suburban literature. Originally conceived to explore the tremendous impact of suburbia on new residents, the research demonstrated just the opposite--that the lives of these people were not profoundly affected by their new suburban location.

In addition, the book challenged the so-called myth of suburbia. The title WORKING-CLASS SUBURB and the opening chapter on the suburban myth called into question both the assumption of middle-class homogeneity and the expectation that this middle-class environment would act like a cultural black hole, swallowing up all social, ethnic, religious, and class variations which came into its gravitational pull.

By examining the lives of 100 auto workers who had moved to Milpitas, California, in 1955 as part of a major factory relocation, Berger demonstrated that the workers moved into an area which became their own working-class cultural milieu and served to reinforce their previous class patterns rather than challenge them or distort them in middle-class directions. Politics, social and civic activity, leisure patterns, and class consciousness all seemed more typical of the working class than stereotyped suburban values.

At the same time, Berger notes the propensity of some of his interviewers to label themselves "middle class" and to identify with or aspire toward a middle-class life. He argues that the suburban (middle-class) myth is one which has been criticized most heavily by those (academics and intellectuals) who are themselves part of that grouping and enjoyers of that lifestyle. He closes with speculation about positive consequences of the suburban myth as a model sought after by working-class or upper-lower-class peoples in American society.

105 Bressler, Marvin. "To Suburbia, with Love." PUBLIC INTEREST, no. 10, Winter 1968, pp. 97-103.

Review essay of Herbert Gans's THE LEVITTOWNERS (see item 109) by a twelve-year resident of Levittown. Bressler argues that Gans's empirical results are limited by his primitive quantitative analysis of questionnaires and interviews, sampling defects, longitudinal research design defects, and participant-observer methodology. He observes that Gans operated on a biased presumption in analyzing "conformity" and "homogenization," overlooking the reality of absolute values in his gratuitous declaration of freedom of association. However, Bressler does concede that Gans's book is indeed very good.

106 Clark, S.D. THE SUBURBAN SOCIETY. Toronto: University of Toronto Press, 1966.

Written in part as a corrective to earlier stereotypical views of suburbia presented by Whyte (item 116), Riesmann (item 16), Seeley et al. (item 112), THE SUBURBAN SOCIETY is a careful analysis of patterns in fifteen communities in the Toronto metropolitan area.

As concerned with process as with a cross-section snapshot of suburbia, Clark discusses "The Process of Suburban Development," "The Creation of the Suburban Community," and "The Choice of a Suburban Home" before he ever gets to a detailed consideration of the suburban population and its characteristics. The author argues, in part, for a selective-migration exploration of suburbanization and suburban impact by asserting that suburban conformity is largely a product of the strength of social, ethnic, religious, political, and family ties suburbanites bring to their new residential situation. Yet Clark observes that the move to suburbia often involves serious costs or deprivations--especially the loss of a previously known urban way of life and form of urban society.

In place of the urbanized individual came the "solitary" family and a new, family-oriented society. However, with community aging, Clark asserts, suburbs become urbanized and the only thing "suburban" about them is their political separation from the central city.

Clearly one of the better serious studies of suburbanization and suburban life.

107 Douglass, Harlan Paul. THE SUBURBAN TREND. New York: Century, 1925. Reprint. New York: Arno Press, 1970.

Taylor, Graham Romeyn. SATELLITE CITIES. New York: Appleton, 1915. Reprint. New York: Arno Press, 1970.

Lundberg, George A.; Komarovsky, Mirra; and McInerny, Mary Alice. LEISURE: A SUBURBAN STUDY. New York: Columbia University Press, 1934.

> Three early studies of American suburbia. Important today for what they tell us about the historical development of suburbia and about the initial reactions of social science to suburbia.

108 Elazar, Daniel J. THE POLITICS OF BELLEVILLE. Philadelphia: Temple University Press, 1971.

> A case study of an older community on the fringe of the St. Louis metropolitan area. Timing of the study places it in the early phases of suburbanization (1940 through 1960). Little of the analysis deals explicitly with the impact of new suburbanites in the community; at the same time the changes and reforms described by Elazar certainly are consistent with other examples of the suburbanization of established satellite cities.

109 Gans, Herbert J. THE LEVITTOWNERS. New York: Pantheon Books, 1967.

> THE LEVITTOWNERS is the single most important study of suburbia yet published. Written in part as a response to the highly critical, antisuburban literature of the 1950s and early 1960s, this book is both the most thorough study of suburban life and politics and, perhaps, one of the very best community studies to come out of contemporary American sociology.
>
> Gans lived in Levittown during the first two years of its existence. He participated in its development and systematically watched events transpire. Unquestionably, the book reflects the biases inherent in his method. It also shares the intimate sense of understanding which comes from direct involvement.
>
> The book is divided into three distinct parts--the origin of the community, the quality of suburban life, and workings of local politics. Because Levittown was a community being formed, the book chronicles and perceptively analyzes the birth of community life--from the initial ideal in the planners' minds, through settlement, to the emergence of indigenous institutions including churches, schools, political parties, and other local groups. After tracing the origins of Levittown, Gans explores the interrelationships among community, family, and the individual, the pressures for conformity, and the process of adaptation. Finally, the author takes a serious look at local politics and the governmental process.
>
> There has been no better study of suburbia than THE LEVITTOWNERS. As new suburbs are born and develop, the importance of Gans's book is again emphasized. The study of American suburbia is handicapped by the absence of other works of this character and quality.

110 Gottdiener, Mark. PLANNED SPRAWL: PRIVATE AND PUBLIC INTER-
ESTS IN SUBURBIA. Library of Social Research, vol. 38. Beverly Hills,
Calif.: Sage Publications, 1973.

This book is a case study of recent suburbanization on Long
Island. When added to earlier studies of this area, PLANNED
SPRAWL provides a continuing description and evaluation of
metropolitan expansion in Nassau and Suffolk Counties. The
book concentrates on Privatown, the largest township in Suffolk
County.

After a general introduction to suburban development and the
suburbanization process in this area, the author looks at the
social patterns of Privatown, local politics, and the submetro-
politan planning process. He identifies three social conditions
in Privatown which seem in part to be a product of the suburbanization process: (1) social segregation, (2) income disparities affecting schooling, and (3) sprawl. In his political
analysis Gottdiener finds local politics and government weak
and incapable of dealing with emerging suburban problems.
Finally, he analyzes the planner process and especially the
role of professional planners in controlling suburban development.

The book concludes not with proposals for governmental reform
but rather with a call for a fuller and more open debate in
the suburbs themselves over the issue of the proper role of
government in suburban areas.

111 Lowi, Theodore J., et al. POLISCIDE. New York: Macmillan, 1976.

New suburbs are born every year. While professional social
science does not provide us with numerous examples of communities in the pangs of birth, the experience of creating
new towns, in the formal or informal sense, is not rare. The
death of a suburb is something else--especially when the act
is one of conscious suicide. POLISCIDE is a fascinating case
study of precisely just such a process.

Weston, Illinois, was out of place from the beginning. A
tract development with illicit funding and low-cost housing in
wealthy DuPage County, Weston still managed to get off the
ground. Then it ran head-on into Chicago's drive to bring
the National Accelerator Laboratory to the metropolitan area.
Weston became the chosen site, and the village quite literally
voted itself out of existence.

Of particular interest to students of suburbia are the discussions of the role of county government in unincorporated areas
and the consequences of eminent domain proceedings on the
area's residents. This is a good book--both for the professional
and the classroom.

112   Seeley, John R.; Sims, R. Alexander; and Loosley, Elizabeth W.   CREST-
       WOOD HEIGHTS.   New York: Basic Books, 1956.

> Based on five years of research in one Canadian suburb, CREST-
> WOOD HEIGHTS is one of the most thorough suburban case
> studies available.   Crestwood Heights, an anonymous community
> now within Toronto, was relatively stable and upper middle
> class in character.   It, perhaps even more than Whyte's Park
> Forest, was both typical of the suburban myth and the cause
> of the myth.

> Because CRESTWOOD HEIGHTS was clearly written as a so-
> ciological study of a suburban community, it is sometimes
> difficult to sort out the concerns of the researchers from those
> of the community itself.   Thus primary organizational features
> are the house and its various functions, time and age, career,
> schools, and the club.   Finally, community beliefs and espe-
> cially reactions to and interactions with experts (social scien-
> tists) are discussed.

113   Sobin, Dennis P.   DYNAMICS OF COMMUNITY CHANGE.   Port Wash-
       ington, N.Y.:   Ira J. Friedman, 1968.

> Sobin's book provides a descriptive case study of fifty years
> of change along Long Island's "Gold Coast."   Formerly occu-
> pied by large estates, the area in more recent years has ex-
> perienced mass suburbanization.   This book supplements Zschock's
> ECONOMIC ASPECTS OF SUBURBAN GROWTH (see item 31).

114   Sternlieb, George S., and Beaton, W. Patrick.   THE ZONE OF EMER-
       GENCE.   New Brunswick, N.J.:   Transaction Books, 1972.

> Plainfield, New Jersey, is a suburban community undergoing
> social and class transition.   Upwardly mobile blacks and Puerto
> Ricans are settling there as the first step in their geographic
> progression out from the city ghetto.

> The book begins with a description of the community, its peo-
> ple, and the changes it is experiencing.   The attitudes of older
> residents are contrasted with those of the newcomers.   However,
> most of the book concentrates on the public finances of the
> suburb.   A detailed analysis of city revenue and expenditures
> patterns is provided, plus a careful look at the needs of public
> education.

> A thorough study of governmental finance in one suburban com-
> munity.

115   Sternlieb, George S.; Burchell, Robert William; and Sagalyn, Lynne Beyer.
       THE AFFLUENT SUBURB.   New Brunswick, N.J.:   Transaction Books, 1971.

> Case study of housing and the housing market in Princeton,

New Jersey. Among the topics discussed are the relationship between housing and land availability and local employment growth. Next, the authors give in-depth consideration to the impact of the extremely high-cost housing market on selected special segments of the population--the newcomers, the "re-shaped" household, the underhoused, and the local municipal employees. THE AFFLUENT SUBURB illustrates the exclusionary consequences of high-cost housing in the suburban market.

116   Whyte, William H., Jr. "The New Suburbia: Organization Men at Home." In his THE ORGANIZATION MAN, pp. 265-404. New York: Simon and Schuster, 1956.

One of the first post-World War II studies of American subur-bia, a classic in suburban literature and the primary source for the so-called "suburban myth." Basic findings of a middle-class, white-collar community are generalized to all of sub-urbia. See also Whyte's THE LAST LANDSCAPE (Garden City, N.Y.: Doubleday, 1968).

For an alternative view of suburban man see John B. Orr and F. Patrick Nichelson, THE RADICAL SUBURB. Philadelphia: Westminster Press, 1970.

117   Zehner, Robert B., and Chapin, F. Stuart, Jr. ACROSS THE CITY LINE: A WHITE COMMUNITY IN TRANSITION. Lexington, Mass.: Lexington Books, 1974.

Case study of four primarily white working-class suburban com-munities just outside Washington, D.C. The most important feature of the towns appears to be the approach of racial tran-sition, and much of what is reported here derives from that fact.

This is a study of lifestyles, of interrelationships, and of so-cial attitudes. After describing the four communities and who moves there and why, the chapters cover in succession thought-ways and lifestyles, social dynamics, personal and community problems, evaluations of the neighborhoods, and local activity patterns.

The authors provide an excellent social and psychological as-sessment of these four suburbs. Little is said about local poli-tics or the economic forces which sustain and impinge upon them.

IV. SUBURBAN DEMOGRAPHY

A. SOCIAL DEMOGRAPHY

118 Berry, Brian J.L., and Horton, Frank E. "The Factorial Ecology of Chicago."
In their GEOGRAPHICAL PERSPECTIVES OF URBAN SYSTEMS, pp. 319-
94. Englewood Cliffs, N.J.: Prentice-Hall, 1970.

Major factorial analysis of the Chicago metropolitan area, treat-
ing suburban areas alone and in combination with central city
neighborhoods. Socioeconomic status, stage in life cycle,
immigrant and Catholic status, race, and population size and
density explain 56 percent of intersuburban variance. The same
five factors also explain 63 percent of intermetropolitan variance. A significant contribution to the understanding of neighborhood and community differences within one metropolitan
area.

119 Cohen, Benjamin I. "Trends in Negro Employment within Large Metropolitan Areas." PUBLIC POLICY 19 (Fall 1971).

General discussion of black employment patterns in major
American SMSAs.

120 Cottingham, Phoebe. "Black Income and Metropolitan Residential Dispersion." URBAN AFFAIRS QUARTERLY 10 (March 1975): 273-96.

Analyzes census data for the Philadelphia metropolitan area in
order to estimate the propensity for blacks and nonblacks to
select suburban residential areas when income is held constant.
Results suggest that blacks are reluctant to leave their established central-city black neighborhoods despite the attainment
of moderate to high income levels. Author also considers constraints on black home ownership and the unique features of
the Philadelphia area.

121   Fine, John; Glenn, Norval D.; and Monts, J. Kenneth. "The Residen-
      tial Segregation of Occupational Groups in Central Cities and Suburbs."
      DEMOGRAPHY 8 (February 1971): 91-101.

      Empirical test of socioeconomic homogeneity in the suburbs of
      eight metropolitan areas which shows that suburban neighbor-
      hoods are little, if any, more occupationally homogeneous
      than central-city neighborhoods.

122   Goldsmith, Harold F., and Lee, S. Young. "Socioeconomic Status with-
      in the Older and Larger 1960 Metropolitan Areas." RURAL SOCIOLOGY
      31 (June 1966): 207-15.

      Comparison of socioeconomic differences both within and be-
      tween central city and suburban areas of fourteen metropolitan
      areas. Data indicates that contrasts within communities may
      be more significant than those between the two residential lo-
      cations.

123   Goldsmith, Harold F., and Stockwell, Edward G. "Interrelationship of
      Occupational Selectivity Patterns among City, Suburban and Fringe Areas
      of Major Metropolitan Areas." LAND ECONOMICS 45 (May 1969):
      194-205.

      Analyzes selective distribution of employed white male nonfarm
      workers in seventy-six SMSAs and identifies two basic com-
      binations of urban, suburban, and exurban selectivity patterns
      which are explained by SMSA age, population size, regional
      location, and industrial base.

124   Goldsmith, Harold F., and Unger, Elizabeth L. "Area Economic Status,
      Area Social Status, and Area Family Life Cycle in Suburban Communities."
      JOURNAL OF COMMUNITY PSYCHOLOGY 3 (July 1975): 231-38.

      Explores the relative impacts of economic status versus social
      status on family lifestyle variables. Data from Prince George's
      County, Maryland (Washington, D.C. metropolitan area), in-
      dicate a strong relationship between economic status and family
      lifestyle, but relatively little relationship between social status
      and family lifestyle.

125   Goldstein, Sidney, and Mayer, Kurt B. "Demographic Correlates of Status
      Differences in a Metropolitan Setting." URBAN STUDIES 2 (May 1969):
      67-84.

      Uses the census tract as a unit of analysis to determine if sub-
      urban residence is associated with different demographic char-
      acteristics. Analysis of data from Rhode Island shows clear-cut
      status differentials with respect to most demographic and social
      characteristics and a full range of status differentials in both

cities and immediate suburbs. The suburban-urban distinction remains valid although the overlap is great and the peripheral suburbs do not have either a broad range of variation or clear-cut differentials.

126 Guest, Avery M. "Nightime and Daytime Populations of Large American Suburbs." URBAN AFFAIRS QUARTERLY 12 (September 1976): 57-82.

Highly significant article which answers four basic questions about the interrelationship of the residential (nightime) and working (daytime) populations of 129 suburbs of more than 50,000 residential population. Analysis is based on 1970 census data on the journey to work. First, most suburbs are both places of work and residence, not bedroom communities or specialized industrial clusters as was previously assumed in the literature. Second, almost two-fifths of the total work force both live and work in the same suburb; variations are strongly related to public transit, housing opportunities, and the industrial composition of the work force. Third, the work force and residential populations of individual suburbs are quite similar.

127 _____. "Population Suburbanization in American Metropolitan Areas, 1940-1970." GEOGRAPHICAL ANALYSIS 7 (July 1975): 267-83.

Outlines the ecological and political dimensions of suburbanization for thirty-seven metropolitan areas between 1940 and 1970. Guest finds little relationship between ecological and political suburbanization. He speculates that as a metropolitan area ages, the expanding central business district creates a central density crater which after some point does not inevitably and progressively move outward; instead, population becomes increasingly distributed in a random fashion around the CBD.

128 _____. "Urban History, Population Densities, and Higher Status Residential Location." ECONOMIC GEOGRAPHY 48 (October 1972): 375-87.

Drawing on the human ecology tradition in sociology, Guest attempts to explain differences in the concentric distribution of higher status neighborhoods by analyzing the population growth in thirty-seven metropolitan areas during various transportation epochs. The streetcar and the automobile are seen as significant factors in reducing the demand for central land use and in contributing to a more heterogeneous metropolitan density pattern.

129 Harrison, Bennett. "The Intrametropolitan Distribution of Minority Economic Welfare." JOURNAL OF REGIONAL SCIENCE 12 (April 1972): 23-43.

Significant article which indicates that in the twelve largest

SMSAs, nonwhite economic welfare is remarkably insensitive to residential location. In contrast, white economic well-being, as measured by unemployment, income, occupational status, and education, increases with distance from the central business district. Author also discusses the policy implications of his findings for the racial integration of the suburbs.

130   Long, Larry H.   "How the Racial Composition of Cities Changes." LAND ECONOMICS 51 (August 1975): 258-67.

Calculates the relative importance of three factors--higher natural increase among blacks, continued black migration, and white outmigration to the suburbs--to the changing percentage of blacks in central city and suburban populations from 1950 to 1970. The steady rate of white outmigration was generally found to be the single most important factor in raising the percentage of blacks in central cities. In the suburbs the modest percentage increase of blacks is due to white and black immigration and higher black natural increase.

131   Martin, Randolph C.   "Spatial Distribution of Population: Cities and Suburbs." JOURNAL OF REGIONAL SCIENCE 13 (August 1973): 269-78.

Attempts to determine whether a density gradient is a more precise measure of the population distribution in metropolitan areas. In seven metropolitan areas author finds a tendency for the population distribution to vary between cities and suburbs, with lower central densities and smaller gradients in the suburbs.

132   Palen, J. John, and Schnore, Leo F.   "Color Composition and City-Suburban Status Differences: A Replication and Extension." LAND ECONOMICS 41 (February 1965): 87-91.

Authors seek to test two hypotheses. First, the white population shows city-suburban status differentials similar to those for the total population, which is confirmed by the data. Second, the nonwhite population does not show city-suburban status differentials similar to those for the total population, which was only partially confirmed by the data.

133   Pinkerton, James R.   "The Changing Class Composition of Cities and Suburbs." LAND ECONOMICS 49 (November 1973): 462-69.

Retesting of Schnore's hypothesis on class composition of urban and suburban areas using both cross-sectional and longitudinal analyses to examine the impact of metropolitan area size and age on city-suburban status changes. Pinkerton finds that the evolutionary sequence is accelerating and that the suburban ring now has higher status, as measured by educational achieve-

ment, than the central city. This is true of SMSAs of inter-
mediate age and size as well as larger and older areas, and
may soon be true in smaller and newer metropolitan areas.
Author proposes a reformulation of the evolutionary sequence
model in which the city-suburban distribution of social classes
no longer varies by the size and age of metropolitan areas,
the middle and upper classes are decentralized in small new
metropolitan areas before they grow and age, and these small
new areas experience the fiscal problems of the older metropolitan areas. See item 136 by Schnore.

134   Poston, Dudley L., Jr. "Socioeconomic Status and Work-Residence Separation in Metropolitan America." PACIFIC SOCIOLOGICAL REVIEW 15
(July 1972): 367-80.

Author hypothesizes that among central-city workers, there is
a direct relationship between income earned and degree of
metropolitan ring residency, i.e., that high-income workers
will live in the suburbs. High positive correlations were found
for most of the fifty-three SMSAs studied.

135   Powers, Mary G. "Class, Ethnicity and Residence in Metropolitan America."
DEMOGRAPHY 5, no. 1 (1968): 443-48.

Examines socioeconomic status of selected ethnic populations
in several SMSAs and relates it to residence in city and suburbs.
Analysis shows that among the various nativity and ethnic
groups studied, suburban residence is associated with higher
socioeconomic levels than city residence. Relative rankings
of the groups remain the same, suggesting that the socioeconomic heterogeneity of the suburbs is due in part to ethnic
migration out of central cities.

136   Schnore, Leo F. CLASS AND RACE IN CITIES AND SUBURBS. Chicago:
Markham, 1972.

This short, tightly written book seeks to test the Burgess hypothesis on urban structure and more specifically whether there
is a general pattern of urban-suburban development which begins with the rich living close to the urban center and the
poor living at a distance and then later evolves into a pattern in which the classes change places with the passage of
time. General data from American cities seemed to support
this argument for the 1950 and 1960 censuses. However, when
race and geographic section or region are considered, the pattern dissolves. See also item 133 in this section.

137   _____. "Measuring City-Suburban Status Differences." URBAN AFFAIRS
QUARTERLY 3 (September 1967): 95-108.

A methodological piece designed to illustrate how different ways of operationalizing social status produce different results. Schnore also explores how the use of SMSA versus urbanized area affects city-suburban comparisons.

138   Schnore, Leo F., and Klaff, Vivian Zelig. "Suburbanization in the Sixties: A Preliminary Analysis." LAND ECONOMICS 48 (February 1972): 23-33.

One of the first articles to present and analyze 1970 census data, now superseded by lengthier, more intensive work. The most significant findings are the slowing of the growth rates of metropolitan and nonmetropolitan areas and the persistence of the suburban trend.

139   Schnore, Leo F., and Pinkerton, James R. "Residential Redistribution of Socioeconomic Strata in Metropolitan Areas." DEMOGRAPHY 3, no. 2 (1966): 491-99.

Another in a series of studies by Schnore and his colleagues which test the hypothesis that certain population subgroups, in this case, educational classes in and around the larger metropolitan areas are changing their residential locations in predictable directions. Results confirm the hypothesis, although the rate of change varies systematically by region, age of the central city, and SMSA population. See also items 133 and 136.

140   Smith, Joel. "Another Look at Socioeconomic Status Distributions in Urbanized Areas." URBAN QUARTERLY 5 (June 1970): 423-53.

Analysis of the suburban population between suburbs and the fringe. Author argues that any study of socioeconomic differentiation must look at a three-way city-suburban-fringe analytical breakdown of the urban population. Smith notes that suburban differentiation is much more evident in metropolitan areas in which central city annexation has stopped. In addition, the article contains a good review of the literature concerning city-suburban status differentiation and the nature of the suburbanization process.

141   Van Arsdol, Maurice D., Jr., and Schuerman, Leo A. "Redistribution and Assimilation of Ethnic Populations: The Los Angeles Case." DEMOGRAPHY 8, no. 4 (November 1971): 459-80.

Relates metropolitan growth and residential redistribution of black, other nonwhite, and Spanish surname populations in Los Angeles County from 1940 to 1960 for a comparable set of neighborhoods ranged by maturity. Findings show that ethnic population increments and redistribution were generally restricted to expanding older neighborhoods and did not occur

at a rate equal to the growth of the metropolis or older neighborhoods; that segregation is greater for blacks; and that assimilation is impeded by the separation and persistence of ethnic
populations in different neighborhood social structures.

B. MIGRATION AND GEOGRAPHIC MOBILITY

142 Bell, Wendell. "The City, the Suburb, and a Theory of Social Choice."
In THE NEW URBANIZATION, edited by Scott Greer et al., pp. 132-68.
New York: St. Martin's Press, 1968.

Author reviews literature on cities and suburbs and draws from
it four alternative lifestyle choices (familism, career, consumership, and quest for community) which might explain a family's
decision to live in the suburbs. Author hypothesizes familism
will be the primary motive. Data generally substantiate this
hypothesis, but also show some career and consumership patterns. Article closes with theoretical discussion of residential
location as a consequence of family desires to achieve its own
preferences for the future (the theory of social choice).

143 Butler, Edgar W., and Kaiser, Edward J. "Prediction of Residential
Movement and Spatial Allocation." URBAN AFFAIRS QUARTERLY 6
(June 1971): 477-94.

Develops a model of factors leading to residential mobility
and then tests the model with data from a national survey.
While the primary focus of the article is on residential movement in general, some of the findings relate to choice of new
residential location defined in city or noncity terms.

144 Droettboom, Theodore, Jr., et al. "Urban Violence and Residential Mobility." JOURNAL OF THE AMERICAN INSTITUTE OF PLANNERS 37
(September 1971): 319-25.

Study of the relationship between perception of crime in residential area and mobility from that area. Data from national
survey of 1,476 metropolitan families in 1967, almost 1,200 of
which were reinterviewed in 1969. Urban crime did not emerge
as a major factor leading either to mobility generally or to
urban-to-suburban residence in particular.

145 Fuguitt, Glenn V., and Zuiches, James J. "Residential Preferences and
Population Distribution." DEMOGRAPHY 12 (August 1975): 491-504.

Significant article in which authors present nationwide survey
data to show that the apparent paradox between public opinion
favoring small towns and actual migration to large cities is
explained partly by the method of asking questions on residential

preferences. In distinguishing preferences by proximity to large
cities, authors find that most people want to live within thirty
miles of a large city. Although respondents expressed a favorable orientation toward rural and small-town life, their
antiurbanism was qualified--they wanted to live close to but
not in a major city. Article concludes with a discussion of
the need to revise public policies to disperse population into
nonmetropolitan areas, since findings indicate no mass exodus
to remote areas or any desire of migrants to return to rural
origins.

146 Goldstein, Sidney, and Mayer, Kurt B. "The Impact of Migration on the
Socio-Economic Structure of Cities and Suburbs." SOCIOLOGY AND
SOCIAL RESEARCH 50 (October 1965): 5-23.

Investigates the role of migration in population redistribution
using special census tabulations for the Providence-Pawtucket,
Rhode Island, metropolitan area. Findings indicate that migration contributes to increasing differentiation of cities from
their suburbs in socioeconomic status, since migrants have higher
status than nonmovers and more migrants of higher status move
to the suburbs than to the city.

147 Granfield, Michael E. "Residential Location: A Comparative Econometric
Analysis." APPLIED ECONOMICS 6 (June 1974): 95-108.

Formulates a model of residential location as a problem of
supply of and demand for scarce sites. Using work trip data
from households in the Buffalo and Milwaukee metropolitan
areas, author finds that socioeconomic variables have replaced
proximity or accessibility to work place as the most critical
variables in determining residential location and that suburbanites as a group have residential preferences significantly
different from city dwellers.

148 Kirschenbaum, Alan. "City-Suburban Destination Choices among Migrants
to Suburban Areas." DEMOGRAPHY 9 (May 1972): 321-35.

Studies migration into all metropolitan areas in 1960 from other
metropolitan areas and from nonmetropolitan areas. The intermetropolitan migrants were of higher socioeconomic status than
the nonmetropolitan migrants. On the whole, both groups pre-
ferred the suburbs, although there was some variation by region
and SMSA size.

149 Ritchey, P. Neal. "Urban Poverty and Rural to Urban Migration." RURAL
SOCIOLOGY 39 (Spring 1974): 7-27.

Study of census migration data which casts doubt on the presumption that rural-urban migrants are streaming into large city

ghettos and disproportionately contributing to poverty levels. Black migrants were found to be no more concentrated in large metropolitan areas than indigenous urban blacks. White migrants were distributed between central city and suburbs in a pattern similar to indigenous urban whites.

150 Sabagh, George; Van Arsdol, Maurice D., Jr.; and Butler, Edgar W. "Some Determinants of Intrametropolitan Residential Mobility: Conceptual Considerations." SOCIAL FORCES 48 (September 1969): 88-98.

Mobility determinants are discussed in terms of the "push-pull" dimensions of family life cycle, social mobility and aspirations, residential environment, and social and locality participation. Intervening factors described include the availability of desirable residences, information regarding residential opportunities, and adequate financial resources.

151 Siegel, Jay. "Intrametropolitan Migration: A Simultaneous Model of Employment and Residential Location of White and Black Households." JOURNAL OF URBAN ECONOMICS 2 (January 1975): 29-47.

Formulates equations of the relationship between residence and work place locations of black and white households and tests them with survey data from the San Francisco-Oakland metropolitan area. Findings indicate that both residence and work place locations are responsive to each other, implying that the decentralization of jobs will result in the decentralization of black residences and that black and white households have almost identical elasticity of demand for housing.

152 Stegman, Michael A. "Accessibility Models and Residential Location." JOURNAL OF THE AMERICAN INSTITUTE OF PLANNERS 35 (January 1969): 22-29.

Article based on national survey of 841 residents in metropolitan areas tests the extent to which accessibility to job and amenities explains residential site selection. Data separated for central and suburban populations. Suburban residents emphasized neighborhood desirability, not accessibility, in site selection and generally were very satisfied with their choices.

153 Tarver, James D. "Migration Differentials in Southern Cities and Suburbs." SOCIAL SCIENCE QUARTERLY 50 (September 1969): 298-324.

Analysis of migration patterns in thirty-one large Southern SMSAs in 1960 shows a substantial volume of migration into, from, and within these areas. Three times as many whites and two times as many blacks moved from central city to suburbs as those who moved from suburb to central city. Migrants to and from these metropolitan areas had higher socioeconomic status than nonmigrants, and city to suburban migrants had higher socioeconomic status than suburb to city migrants.

154   Zimmer, Basil G. "Migration and Changes in Occupational Compositions."
      INTERNATIONAL MIGRATION REVIEW 7 (Winter 1973): 437-47.

      Study of the migration patterns of people moving into suburbs
      and central cities. Data suggest considerable occupational
      mobility on the part of suburban migrants.

155   _____. "Residential Mobility and Housing." LAND ECONOMICS 49
      (August 1973): 344-50.

      Examines residential mobility in metropolitan areas of different
      sizes with particular emphasis on the relationship of mobility
      to selected housing characteristics and particular attention to
      city-suburban differences. Results of a survey of 3,000 house-
      holds show that most moves were not job related and were to
      owner-occupied units regardless of previous place of residence.
      Home ownership varied inversely with size of metropolitan area
      but was more widespread in the suburbs.

V. BLACKS IN SUBURBIA

156   Blumberg, Leonard, and Lalli, Michael. "Little Ghettos: A Study of
      Negroes in the Suburbs." PHYLON 27 (Summer 1966): 117-31.

      Study of blacks in Philadelphia suburbs which shows a direct
      relationship between the 1930 and 1960 residences of blacks.
      Interviews with 379 families indicate that the suburban blacks
      are generally middle or upper middle class, committed to the
      dominant social values, and very much committed to suburbia.

157   Bullough, Bonnie. "Alienation in the Ghetto." AMERICAN JOURNAL
      OF SOCIOLOGY 72 (January 1967): 469-78.

      Compares two groups of blacks of similar education, occupation,
      and income who lived either in a predominantly white suburb
      of Los Angeles or a predominantly black middle-class Los An-
      geles neighborhood on an alienation scale in order to investi-
      gate the psychological barriers to integration. Bullough finds
      that the ghetto blacks score higher than the suburban blacks
      on powerlessness, anomie, and ghetto orientation. Concludes
      that alienation in the ghetto is circular, produced by segre-
      gated living, and tending to keep people in traditional resi-
      dential patterns.

158   Connolly, Harold X. "Black Movement into the Suburbs." URBAN AF-
      FAIRS QUARTERLY 9 (September 1973): 91-111.

      Connolly begins by noting the doubling of the suburban black
      population during the decade of the 1960s and then seeks to
      analyze patterns emerging in suburban black neighborhoods as
      a consequence of this movement. Using census data, the au-
      thor selects twenty-four suburbs for closer examination—some
      with a large black population and others with virtually none.
      Concern is expressed over the proportion of suburban blacks
      living in neighborhoods more than 50 percent black. At the same
      time, Connolly finds black income in the suburbs generally higher
      than black income in the central cities, but still lower than the
      suburban white population.

159 Ernst, Robert T. "Growth, Development, and Isolation of an All-Black City: Kinloch, Missouri." In BLACK AMERICA, edited by Robert T. Ernst and Lawrence Hugg, pp. 368-88. Garden City, N.Y.: Doubleday, Anchor, 1976.

> Building on the more general work of Farley (item 160) and Rose (items 164 and 165), the author looks at the geographic characteristics of one all-black suburban community. Emphasis is placed on the street layout of Kinloch, Missouri, its geographic isolation from its neighbors, and its physical living conditions.

160 Farley, Reynolds. "The Changing Distribution of Negroes within Metropolitan Areas: The Emergence of Black Suburbs." AMERICAN JOURNAL OF SOCIOLOGY 75 (January 1970): 512-29.

> Examines hypothesis that cities and suburbs increasingly have racially different populations by reviewing historical trends in racial composition, analyzing census data on black population growth in suburbs and socioeconomic characteristics of blacks in suburbs, and describing suburbs with increasing black populations. Farley identifies densely settled suburbs near or at employment centers, new suburban developments, and suburbs with public and low-cost housing.

161 Kramer, John, and Walter, Ingo. "Politics in an All-Negro City." URBAN AFFAIRS QUARTERLY 4 (September 1968): 65-87.

> Case study of mayoral politics in an all-black suburb. After describing the creation and early development of the town, the authors analyze the characteristics and campaign issues of mayoral candidates over a twenty-year period. Community politics are described as the "dilemma of scarcity" politics.

162 Nichols, Woodrow W., Jr. "The Evolution of an All-Black Town: The Case of Roosevelt City, Alabama." PROFESSIONAL GEOGRAPHER 26 (August 1974): 298-302.

> Uses the unified field theory of S.B. Jones to illustrate the systematic evolution of Roosevelt City, a suburb of Birmingham. In tracing the suburb's history, Nichols finds Roosevelt City to have taken advantage of its political autonomy to provide adequate services for its residents, but he does not necessarily recommend this method for other all-black suburbs.

163 Rabinovitz, Francine, and Siembieda, William J. MINORITIES IN SUBURBS. Lexington, Mass.: Lexington Books, 1977.

> This short book examines the movement of blacks and other minorities into the suburbs. After generally surveying the national scene, the authors focus in some detail on the Los Angeles

SMSA. While much of the data comes from the 1970 census, some use is made of a survey taken in 1972 of residents in selected Los Angeles suburbs. Four suburbs with a large minority population are given special treatment--Carson, Compton, Inglewood, and Pomona. The authors find that no single pattern effectively characterizes the situation of minorities in the suburbs.

164 Rose, Harold [M.]. "The All Black Town: Suburban Prototype or Rural Slum?" In PEOPLE AND POLITICS IN URBAN SOCIETY, Urban Affairs Annual Reviews, vol. 6, edited by Harlan Hahn, pp. 397-431. Beverly Hills, Calif.: Sage Publications, 1972.

One of several seminal articles by Rose on black suburbia. The author suggests two circumstances of origin for black suburbs--the all-black colony which began as such and remains so today, and the originally white community experiencing racial change. The process of black suburbanization is explored and a total of twenty-three black communities across the nation are classified as "suburban prototype," "working class suburbs," "suburban/semi-rural," and "rural slums."

165 _____. "The All-Negro Town: Its Evolution and Function." GEO-GRAPHICAL REVIEW 55 (July 1965): 262-381.

Rose identifies twelve all-black towns, all but two of which are suburbs, and attempts to determine the effects of socioeconomic development on their form and structure. Four distinct periods of evolution are described: (1) pre-Civil War, arising out of the abolition movement in the North, (2) post-Civil War, (3) the great migration west and north around World War I, and (4) post-World War II, when housing developers were building for the black market. Rose found the ten suburbs to fit a common pattern--dormitory suburbs of mostly blue-collar workers with a higher than average proportion of substandard housing and multifamily dwelling units. Although he discusses possible futures for all-black towns in terms of suburbanization, Rose declines to make any predictions because of the many variables involved.

166 _____. BLACK SUBURBANIZATION. Cambridge, Mass.: Ballinger, 1976.

Major study of the movement of blacks into the suburbs. Rose identifies the main targets of black suburbanization as middle-sized (25,000 or more) communities which often had some token black population in 1960. Two types of such places are identified: the older all-black community and the previously all-white suburb experiencing some racial transition.

The author concentrates on the all-black town, continuing his

previous research on such communities. After discussing the
housing market and environment in black suburban communities,
he treats in detail educational patterns and conditions, social
and economic dimensions of the black suburban population,
the relationship between work situations and black suburbanization, and the quality of life in these communities. He
does not examine the politics of these towns to any great extent.

Most importantly, Rose documents the continuing migration of
blacks from central cities to the suburbs, in contrast to the
dominant white pattern which shows a considerable decline in
city-to-suburb movement.

167 Walter, Ingo, and Kramer, John E. "Political Autonomy and Economic
Dependence in an All-Negro Municipality." AMERICAN JOURNAL OF
ECONOMICS AND SOCIOLOGY 28 (July 1969): 225-48.

Case study of social and economic conditions in Kinloch, Missouri, which emphasizes education as the primary means of
changing community conditions.

VI. POLITICAL CONSIDERATIONS

A. LOCAL POLITICS AND POLITICAL ATTITUDES

168   Browder, Glen, and Ippolito, Dennis I. "The Suburban Party Activist:
       The Case of Southern Amateurs." SOCIAL SCIENCE QUARTERLY 53
       (June 1972): 168-75.

       Reports the results of a survey of Democratic and Republican
       party activists in DeKalb County (Atlanta), Georgia, designed
       to determine the extent and maintenance of amateur political
       activism and the attitudes and motivations of grassroots activists.
       Findings indicate that amateur political organizations are multi-
       purpose and durable, with no major differences observed be-
       tween Democrats and Republicans. Although civic and intan-
       gible rewards are found to be more important in recruitment
       than traditional or personal patronage incentives, the parties
       are more able to satisfy the latter.

169   Eyestone, Robert. THE THREADS OF PUBLIC POLICY. Indianapolis:
       Bobbs-Merrill, 1971.

       One of several volumes published as a result of the City Council
       Research Project at Stanford University. Four hundred thirty-five
       incumbent councilmen from eighty-seven cities in the ten coun-
       ties around San Francisco Bay were interviewed. Unfortunately
       for the study of American suburbia, this sample includes a num-
       ber of places quite distant from the San Francisco-Oakland
       SMSA and clearly not "suburban" in any meaningful sense of
       the term. Most of the books in this series, listed below, do
       not make use of an explicit suburban analytical category and
       thus are of marginal use to the study of suburbs qua suburbs.
       They are, of course, extremely important as contributions to
       the general field of local government and ought to be con-
       sidered essential theoretical materials for those studying local
       government in the suburbs. They are not, however, studies
       of suburbia.

THE THREADS OF PUBLIC POLICY is the one exception. Eyestone breaks down the sample by community type, thus providing highly specific information from several distinct kinds of suburban communities. After creating a model of city policy making, the author examines the problems in each kind of community. While much of the data analysis ignores community type, chapter 6 integrates this factor into the policy model. Causal hypotheses are suggested and tested. The result is a policy model unique to the suburbs of the Bay Area and clearly different from the policy models for either the core cities or fringe communities within the sample. Eyestone's book represents an important step in the development of serious public policy analyses for suburban communities.

Other volumes in the series are listed below:

Eulau, Heinz, and Prewitt, Kenneth. LABYRINTHS OF DEMOCRACY. Indianapolis: Bobbs-Merrill, 1973.

Loveridge, Ronald O. CITY MANAGERS IN LEGISLATIVE POLITICS. Indianapolis: Bobbs-Merrill, 1971.

Prewitt, Kenneth. THE RECRUITMENT OF POLITICAL LEADERS. Indianapolis: Bobbs-Merrill, 1970.

Zisk, Betty H. LOCAL INTEREST POLITICS. Indianapolis: Bobbs-Merrill, 1973.

170   Gilbert, Charles. GOVERNING THE SUBURBS. Bloomington: Indiana University Press, 1967.

Gilbert's study of three suburban counties surrounding Philadelphia (on the Pennsylvania side of the river) is descriptive rather than analytical, historical rather than theoretical. The author provides considerable detail concerning the social, economic, and political patterns of each of the three counties. Chester County was not included. A section on municipal government focuses on six sample communities--Radnor, Marple, Springfield, Ridley, Bristol, and Middletown. An important source of information on suburbanization in the Philadelphia metropolitan area.

171   Greer, Ann Lennarson. THE MAYOR'S MANDATE. Cambridge, Mass.: Schenkman, 1974.

The middle-sized industrial satellite city is not uncommon in American metropolitan areas, yet relatively little professional literature focuses on such communities. Often these satellite cities are suburban in their dependence on the central city, and often they experience massive residential suburbanization. At the same time they do not always want to acknowledge their suburban status.

Greer's book is a political case study of Waukegan, one such satellite city north of Chicago. Her descriptions of the politics of race and the day-by-day pressures of the mayor's office could fit any number of similar places. However, Waukegan is suburbanizing, and the accompanying changes mean that politics there cannot always go on as they have in the recent past. A useful study of the politics of a transitional satellite community.

172 Greer, Scott. THE EMERGING CITY. New York: Free Press, 1962.
_____. GOVERNING THE METROPOLIS. New York: Wiley, 1962.

These two books taken together present related and often intertwined views of the historic role of the city, its evolution, its American characteristics, and its changes and problems in modern society. Suburbs and suburbanization are discussed both as the continued outward expansion of American urbanization and as aberrations in the historic pattern. Urban problems are analyzed from a metropolitan perspective, and their solution is asserted to rest with the political reunification of city and suburbs in metropolitanism. Yet Greer is not sanguine about the prospects of metropolitan government schemes. Drawing on his analysis of the St. Louis experience (reported in Scott Greer, METROPOLITICS, New York: Wiley, 1963), Greer sees an anticity, self-preservationist posture in suburban opposition to metropolitan organization plans.

Both books emphasize the fact of governmental fragmentation in the metropolis. Both books characterize suburban politics in terms of ensuring local autonomy for the purpose of protecting relatively homogeneous, exclusive suburban values and lifestyles (see chapters entitled "The Suburbs: Republics in Miniature" and "The Community of Limited Liability"). Suburban political issues are labeled trivial.

In these two volumes Greer presents numerous testable hypotheses about suburbs, suburbanites, and the way things work in the suburbs. Some are derived from his own research; others emerge in speculative or critical analysis; all are worthy of further empirical testing.

173 Hinden, Stanley J. "Politics in the Suburbs." In PRACTICAL POLITICS IN THE UNITED STATES, edited by Cornelius P. Cotter, pp. 95-115. Boston: Allyn and Bacon, 1969.

Descriptive case study of county politics on Long Island during the 1950s and 1960s. See also James A. Michener, REPORT OF THE COUNTY CHAIRMAN (New York: Random House, 1961).

174   Ippolito, Dennis S.   "Political Perspectives on Suburban Party Leaders."
      SOCIAL SCIENCE QUARTERLY   49 (March 1969):   800-815.

      Ippolito, Dennis S., and Bowman, Lewis.   "Goals and Activities of Party
      Officials in a Suburban Community."   WESTERN POLITICAL QUARTERLY
      22 (September 1969):   572-80.

      > Local political activity in the suburbs was once assumed to
      > be minimal, largely Republican, and rather different from the
      > big urban machines.   Ippolito and Bowman's survey of party
      > activists in Nassau County (Long Island), New York, shows
      > that many well-accepted theories of party leadership can be
      > extended to suburban politics.   Both Democratic and Repub-
      > lican leaders reflect the county's high socioeconomic status
      > but tend to differ according to national patterns in their per-
      > spectives on ideology, commitment, traditional incentives to
      > leadership, role definitions, and party goals.   Both sets of
      > leaders are primarily concerned with success at the polls but
      > are also aware of other party functions and goals.   Authors
      > believe that the activists' emphasis on issues and candidate
      > concerns, which is greater than previously assumed, limits
      > their flexibility and affects the organizational behavior of
      > their parties.

175   Kasarda, John D.   "The Theory of Ecological Expansion: An Empirical
      Test."   SOCIAL FORCES 51 (December 1972):   165-75.

      > Analyzes the relationship between population size and organ-
      > izational structure in 157 SMSAs in order to support empirically
      > the theory of ecological expansion, which holds that popula-
      > tion growth in the periphery of a system is matched by ad-
      > ministrative growth in the nucleus to insure coordination of all
      > activities.

176   Kaufman, Nathan B.   "The Mayor in Suburbia."   PUBLIC MANAGEMENT
      55 (June 1973):   20-21.

      > A discussion of a mayor's responsibilities and relationship with
      > the city manager by the mayor of University City, Missouri.
      > The mayor defines his responsibilities as including the follow-
      > ing: the maintenance of a high level of municipal services,
      > the identification of local problems, and the promotion of ef-
      > forts to apply new technology to community needs.   The mayor
      > must be able to analyze issues and must be sensitive to the
      > impact of issues on different segments of the city.   He must
      > be able to locate the power centers and to get legislation
      > passed in the city council.

177   Lamb, Karl A.   AS ORANGE GOES.   New York: W.W. Norton and Co.,
      1974.

For many, Orange County, California, is the epitome of Los
Angeles suburbia. It is here that Lamb decided to conduct an
intensive study of the political values and behavior of twelve
families. Not pretending to suggest that these people reflect
a statistical sample of suburban or Orange County residents,
Lamb creates twelve pairs of in-depth personal case studies.

The author focuses on general political attitudes, party identification, work experiences, life-styles, and religious values.
Then he explores political attitudes regarding welfare, political ideology, and Watergate in greater detail. Lamb finds
both genuine bitterness and frustration toward government and
a very real sense of hope in these people--hope for integrity
and decency in public life and responsiveness to positive political leadership.

178   Linowes, R. Robert, and Allensworth, Don T. "The Citizen's Association."
       In their THE POLITICS OF LAND USE, pp. 114-42. New York: Praeger,
       1973.

       Description of the role of citizens associations, or formally
       organized neighborhood groups, in suburban politics. Authors
       differentiate citizen associations from traditional civic asso-
       ciations by asserting that the latter have tended to emphasize
       "good government" while the former are primarily defensive
       neighborhood protective organizations.

179   Morgan, David R., and Kirkpatrick, Samuel A. "Policy Variations, Po-
       litical Recruitment, and Suburban Social Rank: A Comparative Analysis."
       SOCIOLOGICAL QUARTERLY 11 (Fall 1970): 452-62.

       Study compares data on the social rank of suburban officials
       for three metropolitan areas--Oklahoma City, Philadelphia, and
       St. Louis. Oklahoma City data differed from that of the other
       two areas in that the social rank of the officials and that of
       the communities did not highly correlate. Authors suggest
       metropolitan area factors also must be considered.

180   Orbell, John M. "The Impact of Metropolitan Residence on Social and
       Political Orientations." SOCIAL SCIENCE QUARTERLY 51 (December
       1970): 634-48.

       In studying the impact of residence in different kinds of areas
       on feelings of personal morale and political efficacy, author
       found that the personal demoralization of low-educated whites
       was increased by residence in central areas, decreased by res-
       idence in suburban areas, and influenced by mobility.

181   Orbell, John M., and Uno, Toric. "A Theory of Neighborhood Problem
       Solving: Political Action vs. Residential Mobility." AMERICAN POLITI-
       CAL SCIENCE REVIEW 66 (June 1972): 471-89.

Highly significant article explores the relationship between
perception of community problems on the one hand and either
local political activity or exit from the community on the
other. Data were collected both for central city and suburban
residents, and the findings are presented in such a way as to
illuminate the city-to-suburb movement of people as well as
the migration of people out of suburbs. Control variables include education level, length of residence in the community,
home ownership, location of friends, and race.

182   Pindur, Wolfgang. "Comparative Recruitment Styles of Urban Legislators."
      MICHIGAN ACADEMICIAN 5 (Summer 1972): 29-39.

Comparison of political recruitment of persons serving on school
boards and city councils in Detroit and five nearby suburbs.
Data indicate that suburban recruitment is largely "accidental."
Role of interest groups is minimal in suburban political cam-
paigns, in contrast to those in the city.

183   Ross, Philip. THE BRIBE. New York: Harper and Row, 1976.

A short, fast-moving journalistic account of what happens
when the Mafia tries to bribe a suburban mayor to insure the
success of a local development project.

184   Schnall, David J. ETHNICITY AND SUBURBAN LOCAL POLITICS. New
      York: Praeger, 1975.

Schnall seeks to explore the role of ethnicity as a factor influencing suburban political attitudes and behavior in the early
1970s. The data are derived from a survey of 525 residents
of Ramapo, New York. Ethnicity was not found to be important in suburban voting. Education and class, not ethnicity,
were found to be most strongly related to suburban attitudes
on local issues. Religion and ethnicity seem to be background
factors influencing party affiliation, but not demonstrating much
direct relationship to overt political behavior in suburbia.

185   Verba, Sidney, and Nie, Norman H. "The Community Context in America."
      In their PARTICIPATION IN AMERICA, pp. 229-47. New York: Harper
      and Row, 1972.

A provocative chapter in the major study of political participation in America. Holding socioeconomic status constant, the
authors conclude that suburban political participation is extremely low when compared to the national population as a
whole. Findings run counter to general political myths and
the observations of some earlier researchers.

186 Wallace, David A., and McDonnell, William C. "Diary of a Plan."
JOURNAL OF THE AMERICAN INSTITUTE OF PLANNERS 37 (January
1971): 11-25.

>   Case study of an attempt at regional planning in the Baltimore
>   metropolitan area. Local politics intervened to render the
>   effort relatively impotent.

187 Walton, John. "The Structural Bases of Political Change in Urban Communities." SOCIOLOGICAL INQUIRY 43, nos. 3,4 (1973): 174-206.

>   Contemporary synthesis of urban politics linking a set of struc-
>   tural changes--urbanization, suburbanization, social polariza-
>   tion, economic polarization, and vertical integration--to a
>   variety of patterned political outcomes. Incorporating sub-
>   urban politics into all parts of his review, Walton specifies
>   the dimensions of segmentation, interdependence, and decision
>   making which he sees as integrating seemingly disparate as-
>   pects of the political process. Walton outlines an anticipated
>   model of political change, in which the courts, federal agen-
>   cies, and wealthier individuals are increasingly involved in
>   social conflict.

188 Williams, Oliver P. METROPOLITAN POLITICAL ANALYSIS. New York:
Free Press, 1971.

>   An extremely useful introduction to the study of local and met-
>   ropolitan politics from the professional's rather than the stu-
>   dent's perspective. Building on economic and geographic models
>   of the metropolis, Williams argues for the use of "access" as a
>   central organizing concept in urban studies. Three types of
>   metropolitan political strategies are outlined: (1) location
>   change, (2) community formation, and (3) coalition formation.
>   Thus the politics of metropolitan areas becomes the politics of
>   homogeneity versus heterogeneity and of accessibility versus
>   the barriers to accessibility. Zoning, urban renewal (recycling),
>   incorporation, and annexation become obvious manifestations of
>   political decision making in this pattern. Four urban problems
>   are briefly explored within this framework--circulation of peo-
>   ple, waste removal, obsolescence, and growth.

189 Zikmund, Joseph II. "A Comparison of Political Attitude and Activity
Patterns in Central Cities and Suburbs." PUBLIC OPINION QUARTERLY
31 (Spring 1967): 69-75.

>   Analyzes survey data on political attitudes and disputes validity
>   of distinguishing among urban, suburban, and rural residents.
>   Author concludes that the nationwide urban-suburban division
>   is the least, not the most, influential factor in explaining ur-
>   ban and suburban patterns of political attitudes and activities.

Political Considerations

B. METROPOLITAN GOVERNMENT AND POLITICS

190 Cion, Richard M. "Accommodation Par Excellence: The Lakewood Plan." In METROPOLITAN POLITICS, edited by Michael N. Danielson, pp. 224-31. Boston: Little, Brown, 1971.

Brief description of the so-called Lakewood Plan by which Los Angeles County sells services to local suburban communities. Program works because residents receive good service and because participation often is made a prerequisite for incorporation.

191 Collins, John N. "Attitudes toward Regionalism in a Rapid Growth Suburb." ANNALS OF REGIONAL SCIENCE 9 (November 1975): 32-43.

Analyzes voter preferences on regional cooperation and consolidation in an unnamed rapidly growing suburb of St. Louis. Although suburban voters are generally assumed to be opposed to metropolitan integration, residents surveyed expressed support for certain operations such as transportation but not for others such as land use and fair share housing. Collins disputes Williams's lifestyle hypothesis because voter preferences in his study are not explained by lifestyle variables.

192 Crouch, Winston W., and Dinerman, Beatrice. SOUTHERN CALIFORNIA METROPOLIS. Berkeley and Los Angeles: University of California Press, 1964.

One of the lesser known, but no less important, metropolitan area studies done during the 1960s. While primarily concerned with the metropolitan concept, its application to the Los Angeles area, and its problems in the practical world of California politics, the authors provide considerable information about the Los Angeles suburbs themselves and about the wider implications of political decentralization in this one urban area. See the following studies for historical background to the conditions described by Crouch and Dinerman:

Fogelson, Robert M. THE FRAGMENTED METROPOLIS. Cambridge, Mass.: Harvard University Press, 1967.
Case, Walter H. HISTORY OF LONG BEACH AND VICINITY. Chicago: Clarke, 1927. Reprint. New York: Arno Press, 1974.

193 Gladfelter, David D. "The Political Separation of City and Suburb: Water for Wauwatosa." In METROPOLITAN POLITICS, edited by Michael N. Danielson, pp. 78-85. Boston: Little, Brown, 1971.

Case study of Milwaukee's conflict with a suburb over one of the essentials of life--water.

194   Hawkins, Brett W.   "Fringe-City, Life-Style Distance and Fringe Support
       of Political Integration." AMERICAN JOURNAL OF SOCIOLOGY 74
       (November 1968): 248-55.

       Attempts to determine factors associated with suburban support
       of political integration proposals by analyzing relevant refer-
       enda since 1945. Findings tend to refute lifestyle hypothesis.

195   _____. "Life Style, Demographic Distance and Voter Support of City-
       County Consolidation." SOUTHWESTERN SOCIAL SCIENCE QUARTERLY
       48 (December 1967): 325-37.

       Empirical test of the lifestyle hypothesis, this time on refer-
       enda on city-county consolidations in fifteen small southern
       areas between 1949 and 1964. Results indicate that familism
       is strongly and independently related to support of consolida-
       tions but that demographic differentials increasingly in favor
       of the suburbs are not associated with suburban opposition to
       consolidation. Hawkins speculates that the lesser social diver-
       sity of smaller areas and the greater influence of elites in the
       South may account for the direction of his results.

196   Hawkins, Brett W., and Dye, Thomas R.   "Metropolitan 'Fragmentation':
       A Research Note." MIDWEST REVIEW OF PUBLIC ADMINISTRATION 4
       (February 1970): 17-24.

       Critique by political scientists directed at the argument that
       metropolitan fragmentation affects municipal expenditure pat-
       terns. Data from 212 metropolitan areas show no such rela-
       tionship.

197   Hawley, Amos H., and Zimmer, Basil G.   THE METROPOLITAN COM-
       MUNITY. Beverly Hills, Calif.: Sage Publications, 1970.

       Reports a major survey of resident and public officials in sub-
       urban and central-city locations within six different metropoli-
       tan areas. The primary concern of the authors is the question
       of suburban versus central-city attitudes toward local govern-
       ment and preferences for different forms of metropolitan gov-
       ernment. While suburban residents expressed considerable dis-
       satisfaction with service levels in their suburbs, these same
       people--not surprisingly--strongly opposed metropolitanism as a
       means for improving suburban service levels. However, the
       authors were not prepared for the levels of central city opposi-
       tion to consolidation schemes. Although this book deals largely
       with the question of metropolitanism, it provides important in-
       formation on attitudes held by suburban residents concerning
       not only the central city but suburban government as well.

198   Lyons, W.E., and Engstrom, Richard. "Life-Style and Fringe Attitudes toward the Political Integration of Urban Governments." MIDWEST JOURNAL OF POLITICAL SCIENCE 15 (August 1971): 475-94.

In testing the life-style hypothesis in an area scheduled to be annexed to Lexington, Kentucky, authors found life-style had no impact on attitudes toward political integration, relative community identifications, preferences for local government service packages, or perceptions of tax benefits. In addition, no support for "social-distance" or "service-benefit" theories about life-styles was found.

199   _____. "Life-Style and Fringe Attitudes toward the Political Integration of Urban Governments: A Comparison of Survey Findings." AMERICAN JOURNAL OF POLITICAL SCIENCE 17 (February 1973): 182-88.

Comparison of survey results in Lexington, Kentucky, and Augusta, Georgia, metropolitan areas refutes life-style hypothesis. In addition, life-style was not related to considerations of social distance or service benefits regardless of the type of integration proposal.

200   _____. "Socio-political Cross Pressures and Attitudes toward Political Integration of Urban Governments." JOURNAL OF POLITICS 35 (August 1973): 682-711.

Uses survey data to determine the relative impact of social-distance, tax benefit, and regime-government orientations, and various combinations of these orientations, on voter attitudes toward two different types of integrative proposals--annexation in the Lexington, Kentucky, metropolitan area and city-county consolidation in the Augusta, Georgia, metropolitan area. Results indicate that cross pressures are strong enough to affect attitudes but that the relative impact depends on the nature of the integration proposal.

201   McDavid, James C. "Interjurisdictional Cooperation among Police Departments in the St. Louis Metropolitan Area." PUBLIUS 4 (Fall 1974): 35-58.

Author studied cooperative arrangements among twenty-eight independent police departments in the St. Louis metropolitan area and found an extensive system of highly regularized informal arrangements. He concludes that the provision of police services would not necessarily be improved by consolidation or formal hierarchical agreements.

202   Marando, Vincent L. "Inter-Local Cooperation in a Metropolitan Area." URBAN AFFAIRS QUARTERLY 4 (December 1968): 185-200.

Analysis of interlocal cooperative agreements among governments in a metropolitan area. Three types of agreements were
identified: contractual, joint, and cooperative. Of the 844
agreements discovered, the overwhelming number involved public works and utilities (354) and police protection (230). Shared
socioeconomic status was found to correlate highly with those
agreements having social policy implications. However, cooperation affecting community lifestyles occurred rarely. Finally,
form of local government--particularly the existence of council-
manager forms--was found to be directly related to community
cooperation in such agreements.

203 _____. "Life-Style Distances and Suburban Support for Urban Political
Integration: A Replication." SOCIAL SCIENCE QUARTERLY 53 (June
1972): 155-60.

With data from nine more metropolitan areas, Marando repli-
cates and extends Hawkins's analysis (see item 194) but refutes
his conclusion that life-style differentials increasingly in favor
of the suburbs are not associated with suburban support of consolidation. Author then goes on to examine various aspects
of urban political integration theory and suggests that the nar-
rowness of the life-style model overlooks the political and
other resources available to persons to protect their life-styles
from changes brought about by city-county consolidation.

204 Mowitz, Robert J., and Wright, Deil S. PROFILE OF A METROPOLIS.
Detroit: Wayne State University, 1962.

A collection of detailed case studies of decision making in the
Detroit metropolitan area. While a number focus upon the
central city, several are uniquely suburban. Most relevant
are the following:

Chapter 3, "Water for Southwestern Wayne County"

Chapter 6, "Detroit's Metropolitan Airport"

Chapter 8, "Harper Woods versus the Ford Expressway"

Chapter 9, "The Twelve Towns Relief Drains"

Chapter 10, "Annexation and Incorporation in Farming-
ton Township"

205 Shepard, W. Bruce. "Metropolitan Political Decentralization: A Test of
the Life-Style Values Model." URBAN AFFAIRS QUARTERLY 10 (March
1975): 297-313.

Building on previous research on lifestyle values models of metropolitan decentralization, Shepard examines one variation of a
market model in the area of metropolitan educational decentralization. He conceptualizes and operationalizes the model,

tests empirical validity of three propositions in 212 SMSAs, and concludes that the adequacy of the lifestyle values model is difficult to assess from findings of weak support for all three propositions.

206 Watson, Walter B.; Barth, Ernest A.T.; and Hayes, Donald P. "Metropolitan Decentralization through Incorporation." WESTERN POLITICAL QUARTERLY 18 (March 1965): 198-206.

Uses two case studies of unnamed suburban incorporation movements, one successful and the other not, to identify the relationship of each of five factors to citizen positions on incorporation--degree of threat or advantage to local values, strength and breadth of individual's involvement with the area, nature and resources of leadership structure, community organizational structure, and campaign effects.

207 Williams, Oliver P. "Life-Style Values and Political Decentralization in Metropolitan Areas." SOUTHWESTERN SOCIAL SCIENCE QUARTERLY 48 (December 1967): 299-310.

A major contribution to the theory of metropolitan politics which attempts to improve existing analytical models as a step toward guiding empirical research and sharpening perceptions of the social values served by the new metropolitan form. Williams rejects the models of international relations, market place, and power structure because they overlook distinctions between centralized and decentralized services. Instead, he suggests a model incorporating suburban communities' lifestyle values, and argues that suburbs will resist integration of lifestyle services but will accept and occasionally encourage integration of system-maintenance services when the issues are perceived correctly. The article concludes with a discussion of the determining factors and the social consequences of suburban specialization.

Williams's model has become the basis of a series of studies which in general have refuted his lifestyle hypothesis. Empirical tests show that a high degree of familism in the suburbs is not necessarily correlated with opposition to political integration, nor is a high degree of nonfamilism in the central city necessarily correlated with support of political integration. See articles by Collins, Hawkins, Lyons and Engstrom, Marando, and Shepard in this section.

C. PARTY IDENTIFICATION AND VOTING PATTERNS

208 Bell, Charles G. "A New Suburban Politics." SOCIAL FORCES 47 (March 1969): 280-88.

An important article which tests the conversion hypothesis of
Republicanism in the suburbs with a study of voting behavior
in Los Angeles suburbs. To his surprise, Bell finds suburban
census tracts to be more Democratic than the county as a
whole, little relationship between suburban home ownership
and political behavior or between residential mobility and
political behavior, and a correlation between the age of housing and political behavior in the suburbs. Bell emphasizes
the need to differentiate between older suburbs built in the
late 1940s and inhabited by Republicans and the newer communities inhabited by Democrats.

209 Hirsch, Herbert. "Suburban Voting and National Trends: A Research
Note." WESTERN POLITICAL QUARTERLY 21 (September 1968): 508-14.

Examination of suburban voting trends in presidential and congressional elections which shows that the suburban presidential
vote follows the national pattern, the congressional vote follows the presidential vote in the same district but is more
stable, and both votes have become more Democratic since
1952.

210 Rubin, Richard L. "The Urban Coalition in the Suburban Era" and "New
Politics, New Democrats, and Suburbanization." In his PARTY DYNAMICS,
pp. 11-83, 98-106. New York: Oxford University Press, 1976.

Rubin assumes that American party politics will become more
and more dominated by the suburban voter and explores the
implications for the Democratic party of this rapidly suburbanizing electorate. Using two Harris surveys of suburban residents, Rubin examines the political trends evident over the
past several decades. An excellent supplement to previous
aggregate studies of suburban voting patterns.

211 Uyeki, Eugene S. "Patterns of Voting in a Metropolitan Area, 1938-1962."
URBAN AFFAIRS QUARTERLY 1 (June 1966): 65-77.

Study of voting patterns in the Cleveland metropolitan area on
referenda and elections in three time periods. The author seeks
to test the Wilson and Banfield "public regardingness" thesis of
local political culture. Three social indexes are used. Social
rank produced the highest correlations with voting in all three
periods, then segregation, and lastly urbanization.

212 Wallace, David. FIRST TUESDAY. Garden City, N.Y.: Doubleday, 1964.

One of the early systematic studies of suburban voting. Community records for the post-World War II era were used to supplement a survey of more than 800 community residents in 1960.
Among the topics investigated were the political behavior of

newcomers versus old-timers in the community, intergenerational
change, voting patterns in national, state, and local elections,
and the attitudinal patterns leading to strong Republican or
Democratic partisanship. A major contribution to the controversy over the political behavior of suburbia which flourished
in the 1950s and early 1960s.

213 Walter, Benjamin, and Wirt, Frederick M. "The Political Consequences
of Suburban Variety." SOCIAL SCIENCE QUARTERLY 52 (December 1971):
746-67.

Using factor analysis, authors attempt to show the influence of
social variety in suburban politics. Residence is found to be
less important in explaining voting than party affiliation, af-
fluence, status, ethnicity, and age. Voting in presidential,
congressional, and state elections and local referenda is found
not to be related to residence. Authors conclude that federal
and state policy must reflect the realities of suburban political
variety and urban-suburban change and stability.

214 Wirt, Frederick M. "The Political Sociology of American Suburbia: A
Reinterpretation." JOURNAL OF POLITICS 27 (August 1965): 647-66.

An early exploration of the political and socioeconomic variety
in suburbia which casts doubt on the Republican conversion and
transplantation hypothesis. Wirt shows that the level of inter-
party competition remains high and attributes differences in
suburban electoral behavior to differences in the socioeconomic
basis of suburbs. He postulates a continuum of suburbs ranged
on lifestyles.

215 Wirt, Frederick M., and Walter, Benjamin. "Social and Political Dimensions of American Suburbs." In CITY CLASSIFICATION HANDBOOK,
edited by Brian J.L. Berry, pp. 97-123. New York: Wiley, 1972.

Through the use of factor analysis the authors document that
American suburbs are not socially homogeneous and that these
suburban differences are related to differences in suburban
voting patterns as well. Besides general socioeconomic status
patterns, the chapter discusses the impact of ethnicity on the
suburban vote.

216 Zikmund, Joseph II. "Suburban Voting in Presidential Elections: 1948-1964."
MIDWEST JOURNAL OF POLITICAL SCIENCE 12 (May 1968): 239-58.

Detailed examination of presidential election returns in 198
suburbs in the Boston, Cleveland, Pittsburgh, and Philadelphia
metropolitan areas which attempts to determine long-term trends
and relation of voting to the socioeconomic stratification of
suburbs within each metropolitan area. Zikmund refutes the

idea of suburban uniformity and the Republican conversion hypothesis and presents findings to show a stable pattern of suburban voting which follows national trends. There is a slight pro-Democratic shift, more evident among previously Republican suburbs, but the rate in a particular suburb is no greater than that in its surrounding metropolitan or rural areas. Socioeconomic patterns correlated strongly with voting in 1948 and 1960, but not in 1952, 1956, or 1964.

217 _____. "Voting Patterns in Detroit Suburbs: 1972." MICHIGAN ACADEMICIAN 6 (Spring 1974): 399-407.

Analysis of Detroit suburban voting in 1972 presidential election and a test of some of Kevin P. Phillips's propositions (THE EMERGING REPUBLICAN MAJORITY, New Rochelle, N.Y.: Arlington House, 1969) regarding suburban voting. Data show no significant change of pattern from that of the 1960s, in contrast to Phillips's assertions.

D. SUBURBS AND NATIONAL POLITICS

218 Danielson, Michael N. FEDERAL-METROPOLITAN POLITICS AND THE COMMUTER CRISIS. New York: Columbia University Press, 1965.

Case study of the politics surrounding the Transportation Act of 1958 and the implementation of this legislation in the New York metropolitan area. The book's primary contribution to the study of suburbia is its focus on suburban response to federal policy making. The author argues that political fragmentation and general conservatism hinder the effective impact of needed national programs in American metropolitan areas. This he asserts is true even when the intent is metropolitan rather than merely central city in scope.

219 Lehne, Richard. "Shape of the Future." NATIONAL CIVIC REVIEW 58 (September 1969): 351-55.

Anticipating reapportionment in the U.S. House of Representatives after the 1970 census, Lehne discusses the implications for the representation of cities, suburbs, and rural areas, and discusses the formation of urban politics. Lehne expected suburban congresspersons and state legislators to be more independent, less party-oriented and, as city problems spread to the suburbs, more willing to resolve urban problems.

220 Murphy, Thomas P. "Urbanization, Suburbanization, and the New Politics." In his THE NEW POLITICS CONGRESS, pp. 209-24. Lexington, Mass.: Lexington Books, 1974.

An analysis of the relationship of the urban and suburban issues in Congress and the influence of the increased number of seats in suburban areas on urban policy.

221   Reichley, A. James. "The Political Containment of the Cities." In THE STATES AND THE URBAN CRISIS, edited by Alan K. Campbell, pp. 169-95. Englewood Cliffs, N.J.: Spectrum Books, 1970.

Narrative description of the changing roles of cities and suburbs in state politics. As suburbanites come to control state government, which in turn controls local government, who comes to the aid of the declining central cities? Reichley suggests that suburbanites behave as if they have more in common with rural interests than urban. A good general description of urban-suburban conflict at the state level after Baker v. Carr, the U.S. Supreme Court decision on reapportionment.

222   "Suburbs: Potential But Unrealized House Influence." CONGRESSIONAL QUARTERLY WEEKLY REPORT   32 (6 April 1974): 878-80.

Contrasts voting records of urban, suburban, and rural congresspersons in 1973 but finds no general pattern of suburban representatives' voting which could be called a cohesive voting block.

VII. EDUCATION IN THE SUBURBS

A. SCHOOL POLITICS

223 Boyd, William L. COMMUNITY STATUS AND CONFLICT IN SUBURBAN
SCHOOL POLITICS. Sage Professional Papers on Educational Organization,
Series no. 04-025, vol. 3. Beverly Hills, Calif.: Sage Publications, 1976.

Analysis of school referenda in the Chicago area.

224 Iannaccone, Laurence, and Lutz, Frank W. POLITICS, POWER AND
POLICY. Columbus, Ohio.: Merrill, 1970.

Highly generalized descriptive study of suburban school politics.

225 Martin, Roscoe. GOVERNMENT AND THE SUBURBAN SCHOOL. Economics and Politics of Public Education Series, no. 2. Syracuse, N.Y.:
Syracuse University Press, 1962.

Solid summary of the importance of public education to suburban communities and the implications of that relationship for
the governance of schools and the place of schools in suburban
politics. Among the topics covered are the suburban environment, the suburban public school, school governance, and the
implications of the central city-suburban separation in public
school systems. Now somewhat out of date.

226 Masotti, Louis H. EDUCATION AND POLITICS IN SUBURBIA. Cleveland:
Press of Western Reserve University, 1967.

Schools and quality education are vital to any suburban community. Along the North Shore suburbs of Chicago, where
superior education is legendary in the New Trier school district, the politics of education can be almost synonymous with
politics itself.

In this book Masotti provides a careful analysis of school politics over a ten-year period. During this time the district voted

twice to reject school board proposals to construct expanded
high school facilities. Finally, in 1962 new strategies plus
increasing enrollment pressures produced a positive referendum
vote. What were the factors leading to the defeat of the
board's plans? What had really changed by 1962–63? These
are the questions Masotti explores. The result is a fine case
study of interest to students of educational systems as well as
those concerned primarily with American suburbia.

227 _____. "Political Integration in Suburban Education Communities." In
THE NEW URBANIZATION, edited by Scott Greer et al., pp. 264–86.
New York: St. Martin's Press, 1968.

Author uses public school decision making in four suburban
areas of Chicago to test theories concerning the viability of plural
communities. Exploration of the politics of school referenda
illustrates differences among the four communities studied. Considerable interlocal conflict was discerned and referenda support varied directly with the apparent distribution of benefits.

228 O'Shea, David. "Suburban School District Government." EDUCATION
AND URBAN SOCIETY 5 (August 1973): 405–36.

Theoretical analysis of relations between schools and the political process in suburbia. Model builds on Easton's concept
of the political system. Data from fifteen Chicago-area school
districts are used to test the model.

229 Smith, Michael P. "The Ritual Politics of Suburban Schools." In POLI-
TICS IN AMERICA, edited by Michael P. Smith et al., pp. 110–30.
New York: Random House, 1974.

Author uses traditional interest groups theory to explore school
politics in suburbia. The respective roles of professional super-
intendents, school boards, teachers, and citizens are delineated.
Conclusions emphasize the " . . . general absence of numerous
interest-group conflicts in the process of policy making in the
community conservationist suburbs. . . ."

230 Wynne, Edward A. GROWING UP SUBURBAN. Austin: University of
Texas Press, 1977.

The suburban schools, asserts Wynne, are the primary socializing
agents for American's post-industrial society. Because suburban
schools are closely tied to suburban society generally, the children of suburbia grow up deprived of healthy diversity and
alienated from the "good life" which bred them. In particular,
Wynne focuses on the administration of schools as both a prime
source of the difficulties he identifies and a genuine vehicle
for change.

231 Zimmer, Basil G., and Hawley, Amos H. METROPOLITAN AREA SCHOOLS.
Beverly Hills, Calif.: Sage Publications, 1968.

Based on interviews of 3,000 residents and 630 public officials
in six metropolitan areas of varying sizes, this book explores
the factors accounting for resistance to change in the organization of school districts. The major analytical contrasts
are drawn between city and suburban residents and among residents of different sizes of metropolitan areas.

Among the topics investigated are use of the schools, knowledge
about schools, participation in school activities, evaluation of
schools, financial support for schools, and views of school reorganization of schools. Finally, the authors look at what
personal characteristics and attitudes seem related to resistance
to organizational change. While opposition to metropolitan
school districts was found among all categories of respondents,
it was most prevalent among suburbanites living in the larger
metropolitan areas.

Parts of this book were originally presented in two articles by
Zimmer and Hawley:

"Factors Associated with Resistance to the Organiza-
tion of Metropolitan area Schools." SOCIOLOGY
OF EDUCATION 40 (Fall 1967): 334-47.
"Opinions on School District Reorganization in Met-
ropolitan Areas: A Comparative Analysis of the
Views of Citizens and Officials in Central City
and Suburban Areas." SOUTHWESTERN SOCIAL
SCIENCE QUARTERLY 48 (December 1967): 311-24.

B. SCHOOL FINANCE

232 Bloomberg, Warner, Jr., and Sunshine, Morris. SUBURBAN POWER STRUC-
TURES AND PUBLIC EDUCATION. Economics and Politics of Public Education Series, no. 10. Syracuse, N.Y.: Syracuse University Press, 1963.

An early case study of the factors influencing suburban expenditure levels on public education. A number of hypotheses
relating tax effort, leadership attitudes, and public attitudes
to school expenditures are presented. Survey data were collected from four suburbs in upper New York state. A complex
scheme for determining influential decision makers on school
matters is devised. Considerable variation was found among
the four communities, both among the communities and among
local patterns of school financing.

233 Campbell, Alan K. "Educational Policy-Making Studied in Large Cities."
AMERICAN SCHOOL BOARD JOURNAL 154 (March 1967): 18-27.

Author studied patterns of differences in central city-suburban
expenditures for education in 216 SMSAs in order to determine
whether socioeconomic differences between cities and suburbs
explain fiscal differences. Findings indicate that the most
important determinant of a central city's expenditures is its
suburbs' school expenditures, although personal income, ratio
of enrolled students to total population, and intergovernmental
aid also explain variation. Noneducational expenditures, home
ownership, and fiscal autonomy were not found to be related
to the level of central city expenditures. Campbell also explored the impact on student achievement of socioeconomic
characteristics and educational resources and found that family
income is the most important determinant.

234 Lows, Raymond L., et al. "Fiscal Homogeneity or Heterogeneity among
Suburban School Districts in Metropolitan Areas: A Case Study." EDU-
CATION AND URBAN SOCIETY 6 (Autumn 1970): 57-65.

In an empirical test of increasing fiscal homogeneity among
school districts in the Chicago metropolitan area from 1950 to
1965, authors found no significant trend toward homogeneity.

235 Sacks, Seymour; Ranney, David; and Andrew, Ralph. CITY SCHOOLS/
SUBURBAN SCHOOLS. Syracuse, N.Y.: Syracuse University Press, 1972.

A major study of public school finance in America's largest
metropolitan areas. Its theme is an old one--city schools face
the most difficult educational challenge and generally have
relatively fewer resources available to meet that challenge
than suburban schools. Sacks and his colleagues provide massive documentation for their assertion. An earlier, shorter
version of this study was "Suburban Education: A Fiscal Analysis,"
URBAN AFFAIRS QUARTERLY 2 (September 1966): 103-19.

236 Smith, Michael P. "Elite Theory and Policy Analysis: The Politics of
Education in Suburbia." JOURNAL OF POLITICS 36 (November 1974):
1006-32.

Reports results of a survey of school board members in six unnamed suburbs in western Massachusetts to support the hypothesis that elite values and role perceptions have a significant
impact on the determination of public expenditures regardless
of the community's socioeconomic level.

237 Treacy, John J., and Harris, Russell L. "Contemporary Suburban Schools
--The Needy?" SOUTHERN ECONOMIC JOURNAL 40 (April 1974):
640-46.

Authors challenge contemporary thinking that central-city schools
are subordinate financially to suburban schools as well as con-

ventional explanations of the dynamics of suburban school growth. They present data on property taxes and costs per pupil for several metropolitan areas in Ohio to support their contentions and then explain the differences in terms of racism, population growth, teaching staff expenditures, and preferences for suburban life-styles. A provocative article that nonetheless overlooks many features of school finance and the important differences between large central-city and smaller suburban districts.

C. RACE AND SUBURBAN SCHOOLS

238 Clotfelter, Charles T. "The Effect of School Desegregation on Housing Prices." REVIEW OF ECONOMICS AND STATISTICS 57 (November 1975): 446-51.

Analyzes housing prices in the Atlanta metropolitan area from 1960 to 1970 in order to show that school desegregation has a significant effect on housing prices and on the demands for housing by whites.

239 Coleman, James S. "Racial Segregation in the Schools: New Research with New Policy Implications." PHI DELTA KAPPAN 57 (October 1975): 75-78.

Controversial article which spawned a debate between Coleman and his critics in subsequent issues of PHI DELTA KAPPAN and elsewhere. Coleman summarizes his analysis from his book TRENDS IN SCHOOL SEGREGATION, 1968-1973 (Washington, D.C.: Urban Institute, 1975), and concludes that desegregating a city school system accomplishes little if it drives whites into the suburbs and leaves the city system nearly all black. He argues both for metropolitan-wide desegregation and for the reassessment of the means and goals of schools desegregation.

240 Collins, John N., and Downes, Bryan T. "Support for Public Education in a Racially Changing Suburb." URBAN EDUCATION 10 (October 1975): 221-44.

Compares recent immigrant black and white suburbanites in University City, a suburb of St. Louis, on their perceptions of and attitudes toward their new residence, its public schools, and its municipal government. Focusing on a vote on a school tax levy increase, authors found no major differences in black and white socioeconomic characteristics or attitudes toward the community, its schools, or its government. Although both blacks and whites strongly supported high-quality educational programs, blacks were more sensitive than whites to the tax burden and did not vote in favor of the increase.

241 Conant, James B. SLUMS AND SUBURBS. New York: McGraw-Hill, 1961.

One of the first statements of the future implications of America's
city-suburban school situation. Conant foresaw what in the
1970s many identified as the increasing opportunity gap resulting from the neighborhood school concept. The author concludes with numerous recommendations, the most important of
which still make sense today.

242 Garbarino, James. "A Program of Attitude Change: Suburban Students
View and Experience the City." CORNELL JOURNAL OF SOCIAL RE-
LATIONS 8 (Fall 1973): 235-42.

Survey of fifty eighth-grade suburban Boston students. Attitudes
toward the central city were compared before and after an
"urban experience" program.

243 Gordon, Leonard. "Suburban Consensus Formation and the Race Issue."
JOURNAL OF CONFLICT RESOLUTION 13 (December 1969): 550-56.

Case study of the influence of the race issue on two school
millage elections in Oak Park, Michigan, a Detroit suburb
which had supported increased taxes until a black community
was brought into its school district. Gordon concludes that
community support of school bonds and millage proposals was
independent of both race and taxes but related to other community developments such as economic and religious pressures.

244 Hermalin, Albert I., and Farley, Reynolds. "The Potential for Residential
Integration in Cities and Suburbs: Implications for the Busing Controversy."
AMERICAN SOCIOLOGICAL REVIEW 38 (October 1973): 595-610.

Article seeks to explore present possibilities for racial integration in American metropolitan areas. Several surveys are quoted
to indicate that white attitudes toward school and residential
integration are shifting in a positive direction. At the same
time, the improving economic situation of minorities makes
residential integration more likely in the future.

245 Ladd, Everett Carll, Jr. IDEOLOGY IN AMERICA. Ithaca, N.Y.: Cornell University Press, 1969.

Ladd's primary task here is to study ideology in American life.
The importance of his study in the suburban literature is that
he chose to concentrate geographically on three distinct places:
the established central city of Hartford, Connecticut, a suburb
of Hartford, and a small town in Connecticut. Methodologi-
cally, the author conducted large-scale surveys, interviewed
numerous community influentials, and systematically studied the
politics and political issues in each location.

When directing the reader's attention to the suburban compo-
nent of the study, Ladd provides an excellent summary of the
major themes in the suburban literature. Although each community receives considerable individual attention, comparisons
among the three appear throughout.

As Ladd himself notes, his suburban community--Bloomfield--
has a special feature which dominated his investigation. By
1967 it was estimated that Bloomfield was more than 12 percent
black--hardly typical of suburbs in the Hartford area or generally. More significantly, racial integration of the public
schools was the major issue to monopolize local politics in
Hartford while Ladd was studying it. The case study is an
important one, especially because of the successful (integrated)
result.

For a more journalistic presentation of a similar situation, see
Reginald G. Damerell, TRIUMPH IN A WHITE SUBURB (New
York: William Morrow, 1968).

246   Levine, Daniel U.; Fiddmont, Norman; and New, Janet E. "Interracial
Attitudes and Contacts: A Sample of White Students in Suburban Secondary Schools." URBAN EDUCATION 5 (January 1971): 309-27.

Authors surveyed white segregated high school students in suburban Kansas City, Missouri, to show that contact with blacks
results in positive interracial attitudes and relationships.

247   Lord, J. Dennis, and Catau, John C. "School Desegregation, Busing
and Suburban Migration." URBAN EDUCATION 11 (October 1976): 275-94.

Investigates the influence of school busing on the migration of
households from Mecklenburg County (Charlotte), North Carolina,
to nearby counties by analyzing growth of the student population and by surveying suburban residents. Results show that
white flight was less than in other southern cities and that
factors other than busing and school desegregation, including
recreation, safety, space, and taxes, motivated respondents'
moves to the suburbs.

248   "School Desegregation and White Flight." SOCIAL POLICY 6 (January-
February 1976): entire issue.

A special issue compiled in response to James Coleman's work
on trends in school segregation. Included are articles by Coleman, Farley, Gittell, and Orfield.

249   Sichel, Joyce L. "White Suburbanites and Integrated Schools: Financial
Support as a Function of Attitudes toward Integration." URBAN EDUCA-
TION 10 (July 1975): 166-74.

Presents new findings from a survey and analysis of voting records in Westchester County, New York, which confirm the importance of favorable attitudes toward integration for financial support of integrated public education. High family income, children in public schools, and support of integration all were found to correlate strongly with favorable voting in school tax elections.

250 Zdep, Stanley M. "Educating Disadvantaged Urban Children in Suburban Schools: An Evaluation." JOURNAL OF APPLIED SOCIAL PSYCHOLOGY 1 (April-June 1971): 173-86.

Case study of school busing found significant improvement in test scores of central-city first grade students who were bused to suburbia. No negative educational consequences appeared for suburban students in the same class.

VIII. ECONOMIC CONSIDERATIONS

A. METROPOLITAN FISCAL DISPARITIES AND THE CENTRAL CITY-SUBURBAN EXPLOITATION THESIS

251 Bahl, Roy W. METROPOLITAN CITY EXPENDITURES. Lexington: University of Kentucky Press, 1969.

> Using 1960 census data and other fiscal data from the same era, Bahl explores the patterns of municipal expenditures in 198 metropolitan areas. He gives special attention to the fiscal aspects of the suburban-central city exploitation thesis.

252 _____. "Public Policy and the Urban Fiscal Problem: Piecemeal vs. Aggregate Solutions." LAND ECONOMICS 46 (February 1970): 41-50.

> General discussion of then-current government policy on alleviating metropolitan fiscal problems, now somewhat outdated because of reapportionment and revenue sharing.

253 Boelaert, Remi. "Political Fragmentation and Inequality of Fiscal Capacity in the Milwaukee SMSA." NATIONAL TAX JOURNAL 23 (March 1970): 83-88.

Murray, Barbara B. "Political Fragmentation and Inequality in the Milwaukee SMSA: A Comment and Some Further Evidence." NATIONAL TAX JOURNAL 24 (March 1971): 113-18.

> Investigates effect of political fragmentation on inequality in fiscal capacity in the Milwaukee SMSA and analyzes the speed at which inequality would diminish if alternative consolidation schemes were undertaken. Results show large disparities which could be significantly reduced by a modest program of consolidating some adjacent suburbs. Murray reworks Boelaert's data with a different statistical technique and unit of measurement, but her results support Boelaert's findings. She then extends the analysis to other SMSAs and concludes that city-county consolidation is best because it reduces fiscal disparities, is politically feasible, and responds to constituent needs.

254   Brazer, Marjorie Cahn. "Economic and Social Disparities between Central
Cities and their Suburbs." LAND ECONOMICS 43 (August 1967): 294-302.

Heinberg, John D. "Economic and Social Disparities between Central
Cities and their Suburbs: A Reply." LAND ECONOMICS 46 (August
1970): 345-49.

Brazer, Marjorie Cahn. "Economic and Social Disparities between Central
Cities and their Suburbs: A Rejoinder." LAND ECONOMICS 46 (August
1970): 349-50.

Brazer presents highlights of her study included in the Advisory
Commission on Intergovernmental Affairs report, "Metropolitan
Social and Economic Disparities: Implications for Intergovernmental Relations in Central Cities and Suburbs." In his comment Heinberg examines Brazer's method of aggregating data
on individual metropolitan areas and other aspects of her methodology and finds no basis for rejecting the stereotype of the
central city-suburban dichotomy. Brazer rejoins that rearrang-
ing and reaggregating the data obscures the relationships sought
by the analysis.

255   Curran, Donald J. METROPOLITAN FINANCING. Madison: University
of Wisconsin Press, 1973.

Curran's book, on a smaller scale, parallels the format of
Williams et al., SUBURBAN DIFFERENCES AND METROPOLI-
TAN POLICIES (item 289). Using tax and budget figures for
communities in Milwaukee County back to the 1920s, the author seeks to explore the issue of resource differences among
suburbs and suburban fiscal exploitation of the central city.

Curran's primary statistical tool is not correlation analysis, but
a rather unique "Coefficient of Quartile Variation." Almost
total reliance on this statistic limits the comparability of Curran's data with other similar studies. Curran finds that nineteen
municipalities--including the city of Milwaukee--show a moderate convergence in spending patterns but an even greater
divergence of tax resources over the past fifty years.

This is an extremely balanced treatment of these highly charged
issues, and the author's caution about either generalizing or
moralizing is atypical in this area.

256   Dusansky, Richard, and Nordell, Lawrence P. "City and Suburb: The
Anatomy of Fiscal Dilemma." LAND ECONOMICS 51 (May 1975): 133-38.

Theoretical development of an economic model to explain fiscal
problems of central cities and suburbs as a set of underlying
technological and fiscal forces and to evaluate the effective-
ness of various corrective policies.

257   Dye, Thomas R.   "City-Suburban Social Distance and Public Policy."
      SOCIAL FORCES   44 (September 1965):   100-106.

      Relates differences in central-city and suburban expenditures
      to differences in their socioeconomic status with a study of
      seven Wisconsin metropolitan areas.   Most significant finding
      is that suburban expenditures for education are greater than
      city education expenditures in only the two largest SMSAs,
      Milwaukee and Madison.

258   Fisch, Oscar.   "The Social Cost of Through Traffic: Contribution to the
      Suburban-Central City Exploitation Thesis."   REGIONAL SCIENCE AND
      URBAN ECONOMICS   5 (May 1975):   263-77.

      Theoretical development of a model to describe the conflict
      between local and through traffic in the allocation of land
      for transportation at the expense of local residential use.   The
      amount of suburban compensation to the central city for the
      cost of suburban access to the central business district is quan-
      tified.   Analysis shows that optimal allocation of land to trans-
      portation never saturates land constraint.

259   Greene, Kenneth V.; Neenan, William B.; and Scott, Claudia D.   FISCAL
      INTERACTIONS IN A METROPOLITAN AREA.   Lexington, Mass.: Lexing-
      ton Books, 1974.

      An attempt to test the suburban exploitation thesis in Washing-
      ton, D.C., and the surrounding Maryland and Virginia suburbs.
      The book looks at public incomes and expenditures, taxes, and
      interjurisdictional transfers.   Depending on how the data are
      calculated, either the city or the suburbs benefit.   The authors
      argue that the technique leading to the latter result is more
      technically appropriate and suggest alternative ways for redress-
      ing the balance.

      This is a very sophisticated economic analysis which clearly
      illustrates the complexity of the exploitation thesis. No attempt
      was made to include private transactions, such as shopping
      patterns, in the calculations.

260   Hill, Richard C.   "Separate and Unequal: Governmental Inequality in the
      Metropolis."   AMERICAN POLITICAL SCIENCE REVIEW   68 (December
      1974):   557-68.

      Nieman, Max.   "Social Stratification and Governmental Inequality."
      AMERICAN POLITICAL SCIENCE REVIEW   70 (March 1976):   149-54.

      Hill, Richard C.   "The Social Stratification and Governmental Inequality
      Hypothesis: A Rejoinder."   AMERICAN POLITICAL SCIENCE REVIEW   70
      (March 1976):   154-59.

      Hill seeks to determine the factors associated with metropolitan fiscal disparities by conceptualizing the metropolis as a social stratification system. Analysis of data from the Milwaukee SMSA shows that (1) governmental inequality is rooted in income inequality among families in the SMSA, and varies directly with residential segregation of social classes and (2) racial discrimination and SMSA size, age, and population density are also important indicators of fiscal differentiation.

In his comment Nieman contends that Hill's use of family income to measure fiscal capacity is deficient as a test of his complex social stratification model. Nieman proposes several other measures which he uses to analyze governmental inequality in thirty-nine Milwaukee suburbs and to draw conclusions different from those of Hill. In his rejoinder Hill questions the validity of Nieman's measures, presents additional data to support his findings, and discourses on the normative perspectives of "public choice theorists" such as Nieman.

261   Kasarda, John D. "The Impact of Suburban Population Growth on Central City Service Functions." AMERICAN JOURNAL OF SOCIOLOGY 77 (May 1972): 1111-24.

Longitudinal analysis of public and private finance in 168 SMSAs which shows that the suburban population has a large impact on central-city service functions.

262   Kee, Woo Sik. "City-Suburban Differentials in Local Government Fiscal Effort." NATIONAL TAX JOURNAL 21 (March 1968): 183-89.

Bowman, John H. "City-Suburban Differentials in Local Government Fiscal Effort: A Comment." NATIONAL TAX JOURNAL 23 (September 1969): 418-21.

Davies, David. "City-Suburban Differentials in Local Government Fiscal Effort: A Comment." NATIONAL TAX JOURNAL 23 (September 1969): 422-23.

Kee compares local governmental expenditures and fiscal effort for central cities and suburbs of several SMSAs and finds substantial differences between city and suburb in all categories of fiscal and tax effort considered. In their comments, Bowman and Davies each take issue with different aspects of Kee's methodology.

263   _____. "Suburban Population Growth and Its Implications for Core City Finance." LAND ECONOMICS 43 (May 1967): 202-11.

Examines changes ·in per capita expenditures of large central cities from 1953 to 1962 to determine if suburban growth harms cities. Growth of the suburban population was not found to be a significant factor, although the number of suburban commuters was.

264 Levin, Sharon G. "Suburban-Central City Property Tax Differentials and the Location of Industry: Some Evidence." LAND ECONOMICS 50 (November 1974): 380-86.

> Although the author hypothesized that the onerous city-suburban property tax differentials have a significant negative influence on the proportion of industry in the central city, data from Michigan labor market areas do not support the hypothesis. Agglomerating factors, proximity to customers, and factor costs, not tax differentials, were found to significantly affect location decisions.

265 Nathan, Richard P., and Adams, Charles. "Understanding Central City Hardship." POLITICAL SCIENCE QUARTERLY 91 (Spring 1976): 47-62.

> Constructs a composite hardship index to analyze the city-suburban relationship of fifty-five large SMSAs, and employs the findings in a discussion of the need for alternative fiscal and political arrangements for spreading economic and social burdens within metropolitan areas.

266 Neenan, William B. "Suburban-Central City Exploitation Thesis: One City's Tale." NATIONAL TAX JOURNAL 23 (June 1970): 117-39.

Brown, Peter G. "On 'Exploitation.'" NATIONAL TAX JOURNAL 24 (March 1971): 91-96.

Neenan, William B. "'On Exploitation': A Comment." NATIONAL TAX JOURNAL 24 (March 1971): 97-99.

Auld, D.A.L., and Cook, Gail C.A. "Suburban-Central City Exploitation Thesis: A Comment." NATIONAL TAX JOURNAL 25 (December 1972): 595-97.

Ramsey, David D. "Suburban-Central City Exploitation Thesis: Comment." NATIONAL TAX JOURNAL 25 (December 1972): 599-604.

Neenan, William B. "Suburban-Central City Exploitation Thesis: Reply." NATIONAL TAX JOURNAL 25 (December 1972): 605-8.

> Neenan conducts an empirical test of the exploitation thesis with data from Detroit and six of its suburbs, and shows that the six suburbs enjoy a considerable welfare gain through the public sector from Detroit, the exact amount depending on frequency of contact with the city. In a series of comments and replies, Neenan and his critics discuss the concept of exploitation, estimations of net fiscal flows, and the appropriateness of his methodology.

267 Pettengill, Robert E., and Uppal, Jogindar S. "Cities and Their Suburbs." In their CAN CITIES SURVIVE?, pp. 57-84. New York: St. Martin's Press, 1974.

The authors use fiscal data from the Advisory Commission on Intergovernmental Relations to explore the fiscal relationship between cities and their suburbs. City patterns tend to show greater per capita expenditures and greater per capita tax effort than the suburbs.

268   Sacks, Seymour. "Metropolitan Fiscal Disparities: Their Nature and Determinants." JOURNAL OF FINANCE 23 (May 1968): 229-50.

Comparative analysis of factors associated with metropolitan fiscal disparities in several large SMSAs which shows that contemporary patterns are due to historical experiences and not necessarily current socioeconomic and political factors.

269   Sunley, Emil M., Jr. "Some Determinants of Government Expenditures within Metropolitan Areas." AMERICAN JOURNAL OF ECONOMICS AND SOCIOLOGY 30 (October 1971): 345-64.

Study of factors influencing metropolitan expenditures in four metropolitan areas. Income level of community residents found to be the best predictor of community expenditures in key services areas.

B. TIEBOUT HYPOTHESIS AND FISCALLY INDUCED MIGRATION TO THE SUBURBS

For the initial exposition of what has come to be called the "Tiebout hypothesis," see Charles Tiebout, "A Pure Theory of Local Expenditures," JOURNAL OF POLITICAL ECONOMY 64 (October 1956): 416-24.

270   Aronson, J. Richard, and Schwartz, Eli. "Financing Public Goods and the Distribution of Population in a System of Local Governments." NATIONAL TAX JOURNAL 26 (June 1973): 137-60.

Develops a mathematical model to illustrate how the system of financing local public services can affect residential decisions and population distribution in the metropolitan area. Empirical test in the Harrisburg, Pennsylvania, metropolitan area shows that the great majority of population shifts went in the predicted direction.

271   Gustely, Richard D. "Local Taxes, Expenditures and Urban Housing: A Reassessment of the Evidence." SOUTHERN ECONOMIC JOURNAL 42 (April 1976): 659-65.

Methodological piece in which the author attempts to determine the extent to which the bias induced by aggregating data affects

the results of previous tests of the Tiebout hypothesis. Two
different models are compared for several suburbs in the Syracuse, New York, metropolitan area. Results confirm earlier
findings and indicate that intergovernmental aid, nonschool
property taxes, and choice of sample can each affect the extent of tax capitalization observed.

272 Hamilton, Bruce W. "Zoning and Property Taxation in a System of Local
Governments." URBAN STUDIES 12 (June 1975): 205-11.

Theoretical discussion and extension of the Tiebout hypothesis
on the provision of public services in a multijurisdictional urban
fiscal system.

273 Haskell, Mark A., and Leshinski, Stephen. "Fiscal Influences on Residential Choice: A Study of the New York Region." QUARTERLY RE-
VIEW OF ECONOMICS AND BUSINESS 9 (Winter 1969): 47-55.

Attempts to measure fiscal residua, defined as the algebraic
difference between taxes paid and benefits received from public
services, for families in 280 selected New York City suburbs
in 1965. Fiscal residua were found to vary with per pupil
educational expenditures.

274 Murray, Barbara B. "Central City Expenditures and Out-Migration to the
Fringe." LAND ECONOMICS 45 (November 1969): 471-74.

Examines the level and composition of central-city expenditures,
excluding education, as one possible set of determinants of the
number of migrants from the central city to the suburbs. Author concludes that central-city expenditures, particularly police and fire expenditures per capita, were a significant factor
in the decision to move to the suburbs except for the lowest
and highest income groups.

275 Oates, Wallace E. "The Effects of Property Taxes and Local Public Spend-
ing on Property Values: An Empirical Study of Tax Capitalization and the
Tiebout Hypothesis." JOURNAL OF POLITICAL ECONOMY 77 (November-
December 1966): 957-71.

Confirms the Tiebout hypothesis using data from fifty-three New
Jersey suburbs of New York City.

C. GENERAL URBAN ECONOMICS

276 Bradford, David F., and Kelejian, Harry H. "An Economic Model of the
Flight to the Suburbs." JOURNAL OF POLITICAL ECONOMY 81 (May-June
1973): 566-89.

Parvin, Joseph. "The Effect of Race on the Flight to the Suburbs."
JOURNAL OF POLITICAL ECONOMY 83 (August 1975): 865.

Bradford and Kelejian devise and test econometric models which
confirm that middle-class migration to the suburbs is causing
problems for the central cities. Their principal finding is that
race is not a significant factor in residential location decisions.
Parvin reruns the regression analysis with the white middle class
as the dependent variable and finds race to be a significant
factor in influencing that class's residential location decisions.

277 Chinitz, Benjamin, ed. CITY AND SUBURB. Englewood Cliffs, N.J.:
Prentice-Hall, 1964.

An older collection of essays emphasizing the economic aspects
of metropolitan growth. Though more metropolitan than suburban in scope, the subject matter obviously has relevance to
suburban conditions as well as those of the central city. The
original essays in the collection are Chinitz, "City and Suburb,"
and Arnold R. Weber, "Labor Market Perspectives of the New
City."

278 Colman, William G. CITIES, SUBURBS, AND STATES. New York: Free
Press, 1975.

Colman's book is not really a study of suburbia, but rather a
detailed examination of central city-suburban interrelations.
One of the author's primary emphases is the importance of
state government in urban affairs. At the end of his first
chapter Colman lists several factors he feels are the sources
of America's urban ills. Of these, the solution to only two
of these--school integration and suburban zoning--could rest
exclusively in the hands of local governments. Three--racism,
crime, and rural-to-urban migration patterns--are national social movements. One, legislative apportionment, is essentially
a state problem, and the others--housing, police, highway
programs, and underfunding urban-oriented federal programs--
are the result of decisions in Washington.

While Colman seems antisuburban throughout ("Feathering the
Suburban Fiscal Nest"), this volume does contain considerable
hard data on suburbs. Similarly, it provides one of the most
readable statements of the fiscal version of the suburban exploitation thesis. Clearly, the most central focus of the book
is the central city, its problems, and proposals for the solution
of those problems.

An earlier and shorter volume covering some of the same material is David L. Birch, THE ECONOMIC FUTURE OF CITY
AND SUBURB (New York: Committee for Economic Development, 1970).

279   Cox, Kevin R. CONFLICT, POWER AND POLITICS IN THE CITY. New
      York: McGraw-Hill, 1973.

      This compact book is an excellent introduction to the political
      geography of American metropolitan areas. Building on eco-
      nomic theory, Cox explores the spatial implications of individ-
      ual "maximization" decisions and the externalities these deci-
      sions create. In three very tight chapters the author describes
      the territorial organization of metropolitan areas, the conse-
      quences of metropolitan fragmentation, and spatial conflict
      within the city. He closes with a look at the policy implica-
      tions of these conditions. A significant theoretical and analyt-
      ical contribution to the suburban exploitation literature.

      For an alternative view of many of these same topics, see
      Robert L. Bish, THE PUBLIC ECONOMY OF METROPOLITAN
      AREAS (Chicago: Markham, 1971).

280   Cuthbertson, Ida D. "Fiscal Impact of New Town and Suburban Develop-
      ment." URBAN LAND 35 (January 1976): 5-12.

      A careful study of the public finance of two communities in Fairfax
      County, Virginia. Reston, because of its mixed residential-
      industrial commercial character, generates a revenue surplus
      while West Springfield, the more traditional suburb,does not.

281   Downes, Bryan T. "Suburban Differentiation and Municipal Policy Choices."
      In COMMUNITY STRUCTURE AND DECISION-MAKING, edited by Terry
      N[ichols]. Clark, pp. 243-67. San Francisco: Chandler, 1968.

      Downes develops a four-category classification scheme for sub-
      urbs based on their public expenditure patterns and then relates
      this typology to (1) social, economic, and political character-
      istics of the communities, (2) city councilmen characteristics,
      and (3) council procedures. The data analysis of thirty-seven
      St. Louis suburbs is secondary to creation of labeling.

282   Firestine, Robert E. "The Impact of Reapportionment upon Local Govern-
      ment Aid Receipts within Large Metropolitan Areas." SOCIAL SCIENCE
      QUARTERLY 54 (September 1973): 394-402.

      In a test of the impact of reapportionment on changes in per
      capita aid receipts of local governments in large metropolitan
      areas, author finds reapportionment had a barely detectable
      positive effort on state-distributed aid, but cautions that any
      conclusions are limited by aggregate analysis.

283   Gylys, Julius A. "Economic Problems in Provision of Police Services with-
      in a Metropolitan Setting." SOCIAL SCIENCE 44 (April 1969): 76-80.

Theoretical determination of the most cost-effective method of providing police services by small overlapping jurisdictions in a metropolitan area.

284 Harrison, Bennett. URBAN ECONOMIC DEVELOPMENT: SUBURBANIZA-TION, MINORITY OPPORTUNITY AND THE CONDITION OF THE CEN-TRAL CITY. Washington, D.C.: Urban Institute, 1974.

This book seeks to explore how the suburbs affect the capacity of the central city to provide economically for its residents. Harrison doubts that the movement of industry and jobs to the suburbs is the primary source of central-city ills. Rather, he argues, these are a product of the long-term dynamics of the national economy. The author asserts that the failure to adjust to these national patterns, not suburbanization, constitutes the most serious threat to the viability of the central city.

285 Holtmann, A.G. "Migration to the Suburbs, Human Capital and City In-come Tax Losses: A Case Study." NATIONAL TAX JOURNAL 21 (Sep-tember 1968): 326-31.

Formulates an equation for the process of dynamic deterioration of the central city and tests it in the Detroit metropolitan area.

286 Rothenberg, Jerome. "Strategic Interaction and Resource Allocation in Metropolitan Intergovernmental Relations." AMERICAN ECONOMIC RE-VIEW 59 (May 1969): 494-503.

Theoretical development of a mathematical model of the con-flicting factors which influence residential and industrial loca-tion decisions in metropolitan areas.

287 Stanback, Thomas M., and Knight, Richard V. SUBURBANIZATION AND THE CITY. Montclair, N.J.: Allanheld, Osmun and Co., 1976.

A major, original, and highly authoritative study of the eco-nomics of American suburbia. Data from ten metropolitan areas are analyzed: Atlanta, Baltimore, Boston, Cleveland, Denver, Houston, New Orleans, New York, Philadelphia, and St. Louis.

The study emphasizes the labor market dynamics behind suburban growth. Contrasting residential location versus employment location, the authors estimate that about two-thirds of all sub-urban income still comes from the central cities. Despite the movement of jobs to the suburbs, the authors argue that this dependence on central-city employment will continue for some time. The reason, they assert, is because manufacturing and warehousing--previously the leaders in the industrial flight to the suburbs--are becoming less and less "economically feasible" in the suburbs with rising land costs and taxes. In addition, the labor pool for such industries in the suburbs is limited and not likely to expand significantly in the near future. The likely result is not the resurgence of the city, but the further dispersal of economic enterprises into smaller, free-standing cities and rural areas. Among the specialized topics discussed are transportation influences, industrial characteristics, occupational characteristics and commuter flows, labor market characteristics, labor market flows, and the problems of the unskilled worker in cities and suburbs.

Stanback and Knight have made an extremely important contribution to the understanding of suburbia and central city-suburban interrelationships.

288 Stephens, G. Ross. "The Suburban Impact of Earnings Tax Policies." NATIONAL TAX JOURNAL 22 (September 1969): 313-33.

Using a theoretical model, the author analyzes the impact of alternative tax-levying policies on the metropolis. The model metropolis contains a central city and eight different types of suburbs.

289 Williams, Oliver P., et al. SUBURBAN DIFFERENCES AND METROPOLITAN POLICIES. Philadelphia: University of Pennsylvania Press, 1965.

One of the best studies yet done comparing suburbs within one metropolitan area. Looking at 225 suburban places on the Pennsylvania side of Philadelphia's suburbia, the authors use 1950 and 1960 census data, 1959-60 fiscal data, plus 1952-60 election data to identify differences among suburban communities and to analyze relationships with revenue, spending, and electoral patterns. The book focuses on one central hypothesis:

"We hypothesize that levels of expenditure and their distribution among alternative functions of government represent policy choices reflective of community values and that these values are structured by, and correlate with, certain measurable social, economic, and political attributes of a community." (p. 77)

This hypothesis is then tested by correlating expenditures for municipal programs, school revenues, tax policies, and land use policies against socioeconomic data for each community.

Finally, a brief survey was made of both residents and public officials in sixteen suburbs. General sociopolitical attitudes are compared between the two groups as are attitudes toward local services, public policies, and community change.

In their closing chapters the authors explore the implications of suburban differences for metropolitan integration. They highlight three major metropolitan problems derived from areal specialization or suburban differentiation: (1) maintaining the services necessary for the continuance of areal specialization, (2) the unequal distribution of resources and services among suburbs, and (3) boundary relationships. They conclude that the prospects for effective metropolitan government are shaky at best.

290 Wood, Robert C. 1400 GOVERNMENTS. Cambridge, Mass.: Harvard University Press, 1961.

This is one of the last of the New York Metropolitan Region Study volumes, which also included ANATOMY OF A ME-TROPOLIS (item 46). In 1400 GOVERNMENTS, Wood explores the political economy of the area--how local governments raise and spend their money. Most importantly, the author provides an extremely sophisticated analysis of the factors which influence the levels of public spending in different local communities within the metropolis. The correlation and factor analyses presented are comparable or superior to any similar work published in the subsequent fifteen years.

After identifying the dominant patterns for the region, Wood looks at the pressures emerging on the public sector economy. (Here his discussion, "The Segregation of Resources and Needs," serves as an early warning of conditions which would lead to the "suburban exploitation" thesis a decade later.) Next Wood examines the responses generated in the metropolitan area to cope with these pressures. Finally, the metropolitan special districts come under Wood's scrutiny.

Considering all that has happened to the political economy of New York in the 1970s, 1400 GOVERNMENTS must be seen as a highly perceptive and prophetic book.

IX. SOCIOLOGICAL FACTORS

A. SOCIAL CHARACTERISTICS AND BEHAVIOR

291 Baldassare, Mark, and Fischer, Claude S. "Suburban Life: Powerlessness and Need for Affiliation." URBAN AFFAIRS QUARTERLY 10 (March 1975): 314-26.

Reexamines findings of two surveys conducted during the 1960s to determine if personality differences are related to city or suburban residence. Authors conclude that no substantial evidence was found to support hypothesis that suburban residents have a higher need for affiliation and that city residents have more feelings of powerlessness.

292 Birch, David L., et al. "Individuals and Households." In their PATTERNS OF URBAN CHANGE: THE NEW HAVEN EXPERIENCE, pp. 25-35. Lexington, Mass.: D.C. Heath, 1974.

This chapter outlines some of the changes that have taken place in the New Haven metropolitan region. The authors consider the factors determining the location of people and the migration to the suburbs. They observe that transportation availability and work place proximity no longer dominate residential choice. They conclude that sociological and aesthetic considerations such as race, social status, and the age of neighborhoods are the factors that influence choice.

293 Bogart, Leo, and Orenstein, Frank E. "Mass Media and Community Identity in an Interurban Setting." JOURNALISM QUARTERLY 42 (Spring 1965): 179-88.

Authors surveyed residents of an unnamed suburb on their newspaper reading and television watching habits in order to test hypothesis that suburbanites' mass media preferences will reflect their social, working, and consumer behavior. Hypothesis was confirmed for newspaper reading but not television watching.

294 Boskoff, Alvin. "Social and Cultural Patterns in a Suburban Area: Their Significance for Urban Change in the South." JOURNAL OF SOCIAL ISSUES 22 (January 1966): 85-100.

Summarizes and interprets a series of studies done in a suburban Atlanta zone. Topics covered include social and cultural heterogeneity, formal family associational patterns, contacts with relatives, and local and national electoral behavior.

295 Bruce-Biggs, B. "Gasoline Prices and the Suburban Way of Life." PUBLIC INTEREST, no. 37, Fall 1974, pp. 131-36.

Writing during the Arab oil embargo of 1973-74, Bruce-Biggs predicted that the suburban way of life would not be threatened and that suburbanization would continue because car ownership costs are not sensitive to gasoline prices.

296 Dobriner, William M. CLASS IN SUBURBIA. Englewood Cliffs, N.J.: Prentice-Hall, 1963.

CLASS IN SUBURBIA is Dobriner's second important contribution to the suburban literature (see item 16 for the other). It is made up of four rather distinct parts: (1) a general discussion of class in suburbia, (2) an updating of the author's previous work on Levittown, (3) the reprint of his article "The Natural History of a Reluctant Suburb," and (4) a generalized description of the structure and development of metropolitan areas.

Perhaps the most significant and lasting contribution here is contained in the first section, the discussion of class in suburbia. In his preface Dobriner refers to his 1958 statement that researchers other than social scientists attribute middle-class behavior to suburbia. In the discussion of class in suburbia, Dobriner explores these issues and demonstrates the class diversity of suburbs and the subtle distinctions of ethnicity, religion, and history which differentiate suburban communities.

297 Eaton, William W., Jr. "Residence, Social Class, and Schizophrenia." JOURNAL OF HEALTH AND SOCIAL BEHAVIOR 15 (December 1974): 289-99.

Relates incidence of schizophrenia to class and residence. Data show suburbanites have about half the rate of illness of central-city residents.

298 Hodge, Robert W., and Treiman, Donald J. "Social Participation and Social Status." AMERICAN SOCIOLOGICAL REVIEW 33 (Ocotber 1968): 722-40.

Assesses the effect of one method of recruitment to voluntary organizations, the intergenerational transmission of social participation patterns, with a survey of residents in an unnamed

suburb of Washington, D.C. Findings show that transmission
is high for both females and males but the different aspects of
social participation studied are not explained by social status.
Results were not confirmed when Detroit blacks were similarly
surveyed.

299   Hodges, Harold M., Jr. "Peninsula People: Social Stratification in a
      Metropolitan Complex." In NEIGHBORHOOD, CITY AND METROPOLIS,
      edited by Robert Gutman and David Popenoe, pp. 309-33. New York:
      Random House, 1970.

      Based on more than 3,000 "heads of households" in the San
      Francisco area, this paper identifies six distinct social classes
      among suburbanites in the Bay Area. Each group is described
      in detail in terms of their general characteristics and most
      typical examples. The article provides useful evidence of the
      social diversity within the suburbs of just one metropolitan
      area.

300   Humphrey, Craig R., and Krout, John A. "Traffic and the Suburban
      Highway Neighbor." TRAFFIC QUARTERLY 24 (October 1975): 593-613.

      Authors sought to measure the perception and consequences of
      the environmental impacts of traffic on heavily used high-speed
      roads for families living near such roads in four suburbs. Noise
      was found to be the most annoying impact and exhaust smells
      the least. The degree of annoyance was related to several
      factors, including concern for adverse effect on property values,
      distance from the road, and use of outdoor recreation facilities.
      Socioeconomic status was one of several factors not found to
      be related to annoyance.

301   James, Gilbert. "Community Structure and Anomia." In THE NEW UR-
      BANIZATION, edited by Scott Greer et al., pp. 189-97. New York:
      St. Martin's Press, 1968.

      Urban-suburban comparison of anomie indicators in the St. Louis
      metropolitan area. Author suggests difference related to life-
      style contracts in typical central city and suburban living en-
      vironments.

302   Jung, L. Shannon. "The Shape of American Space." RELIGION IN
      LIFE 44 (Spring 1975): 36-46.

      General discussion of the phenomenon of walled or fortress
      suburbs in terms of the concept of personal spatial dynamics.

303   Kaplan, Samuel. THE DREAM DEFERRED. New York: Seabury Press, 1976.

      Excellent journalistic account of life and politics in suburbia.

Limited by the eastern, and especially the Long Island, environment in which the story takes place (Port Washington, New York). Good on local color and readability; not as good on proposing solutions for the problems identified.

304 Koehler, Cortus T. "A Comparative Study of Three Suburban Malls: The Influence of Physical Environment on Pedestrian Behavior." JOURNAL OF ENVIRONMENTAL SYSTEMS 3 (Spring 1973): 17-25.

Authors surveyed shoppers in three suburban Los Angeles shopping malls in order to learn which of three mall forms is the most effective in generating pedestrian activity on the mall. Data show that the proper environmental context will induce people to shop by foot as well as by car.

305 Morgan, David R. "Community Social Rank and Attitudes toward Suburban Living." SOCIOLOGY AND SOCIAL RESEARCH 55 (July 1971): 401-13.

Examines attitudes toward suburban living in five Oklahoma City suburbs to determine if responses vary in accordance with community social status. Meaningful differences were found, with lower-status suburbanites preferring the small town aspects of suburban life to the "bigness" of the city, and the upper-status suburbanites more concerned with suburban amenities and lower taxes.

306 Zehner, Robert B. "Neighborhood and Community Satisfaction in New Towns and Less Planned Suburbs." JOURNAL OF THE AMERICAN INSTITUTE OF PLANNERS 37 (November 1971): 379-85.

Comparative study of two planned communities--Columbia, Maryland, and Reston, Virginia--and two similar, unplanned suburbs. Primary focus was on the question of neighborhood or community satisfaction. Planned communities consistently scored higher than suburbs; however, in overall satisfaction with area the suburbs also scored very well. Suburbs showed poorest in neighborhood quietness, play areas for children, and friendly neighbors. On the other hand, the suburbs scored higher than the planned communities on the basis of school quality.

307 Zikmund, Joseph II. "Do Suburbanites Use the Central City?" JOURNAL OF THE AMERICAN INSTITUTE OF PLANNERS 37 (May 1971): 192-95.

Article explores suburbanites' patterns of interaction with the central city. Questions answered deal with how often suburbanites go to the central city to take advantage of the city's shopping or cultural advantages and any differences among suburbanites in their use of the central city. Center city visitation was found to be directly related to commuting into the city for work and to other socioeconomic factors.

B. FAMILY AND CHILDREN

308   Balkin, Esther, et al. "Attitudes toward Classroom Discussions of Death
and Dying among Urban and Suburban Children." OMEGA: JOURNAL
OF DEATH AND DYING 7, no. 2 (1976): 183-89.

A brief study of attitudes expressed by fifty suburban and fifty
urban children about the appropriateness of the discussion of
death in the classroom. Suburban children seemed more willing
to have such discussions.

309   Goodwin, Leonard. "How Suburban Families View the Work Orientations
of the Welfare Poor: Problems in Social Stratification and Social Policy."
SOCIAL PROBLEMS 19 (Winter 1972): 337-48.

Reports data from a survey of 210 suburban families, 220 welfare mothers in a special program, plus 267 other welfare
mothers, all in and around Baltimore. Comparison of attitudes
of each survey group regarding "work ethic" and general self-
confidence. Data show considerable misperception by suburbanites of welfare mothers' commitment to work ethic.

310   Gordon, Richard E., et al. THE SPLIT-LEVEL TRAP. New York: Bernard
Geis Associates, 1960.

Gordon and his associates provide a picture of psychiatric aspects of life in suburbia. Through numerous case studies the
authors explore common personality and social problems. Chapters focus particularly on major relational situations and the
tensions they create: young wives, child rearing, young hus-
bands, marriage and divorce, children and adolescents, singles,
and the elderly. If the tone of the book emphasizes the problems of suburban life, the reader must remember that a prac-
ticing psychiatrist is likely to get a somewhat biased perspective on the environment in which he or she practices.

311   LeMasters, E.E. BLUE-COLLAR ARISTOCRATS. Madison: University of
Wisconsin Press, 1975.

Provides a well-conceived and well-executed illustration of
blue-collar social life in a suburban environment. LeMasters
describes the results of four years of observer-participation at
the Oasis Bar, a regular hangout for middle-income, working-
class white males in a suburb of Madison, Wisconsin. He
writes with wit and style and integrates his quotes and stories
into a well-established base in the traditional suburban literature. Among the topics covered are work, marriage, male-
female relations, children and family, tavern social life, drink-
ing and alcoholism, and attitudes on politics, race, and religion.
A good case study in an area where much needs to be done.

312 Levine, Daniel U. "Contrasting Educative Environments in the Metropolitan Area." EDUCATIONAL HORIZONS 48 (Fall 1969): 5-12.

General discussion of the differences between the nonschool environments of children in center city ghettos and suburbs, the myth of noncaring ghetto parents, and the roots of discipline problems in the suburbs.

313 Licht, M. "Some Automotive Play Activities of Suburban Teenagers." NEW YORK FOLKLORE QUARTERLY 30 (March 1974): 44-65.

Draws representative impressionistic sketch of teenage car games, pranks, and other activities from surveys and interviews with teenagers and relevant adults in various New York State suburbs. Author concludes that in a suburban environment largely determined by the use of a car, in which the nondriver is not a functional adult, the years of clearest transition from childhood to adulthood are the initial years of driving.

314 Lopata, Helena Z. OCCUPATION: HOUSEWIFE. New York: University Press, 1971.

Much has been made of the traditional role of the housewife--both in modern sociological literature and in the early writings on suburbia. William Whyte emphasized the impact of suburbanization on the family and on local social life. More recently, the works of contemporary feminists have held up the housewife role to critical analysis and often bitter ridicule.

Lopata explores the situation of the suburban housewife in great detail. Based primarily on a sample of women in twelve Chicago suburbs, this study provides concrete information on a topic subject to a great deal of speculation and wishful thinking. Among the subjects explored are the female life cycle plus five basic roles for women: wife, housewife, mother, neighbor, and friend.

This is an extremely important book for the study of women in their changing twentieth-century roles. It is also an important contribution to research on life in suburbia.

315 Omvig, Clayton P., and Thomas, Edward G. "Vocational Interests of Affluent Suburban Students." VOCATIONAL GUIDANCE QUARTERLY 23 (September 1974): 10-16.

Descriptive study of vocational preferences of 101 white ninth-grade students in an affluent suburban community.

316 Shappell, Dean L., and Hall, Lacy G. "Perceptions of the World of Work: Inner City versus Suburbia." JOURNAL OF COUNSELING PSYCHOLOGY 18 (January 1971): 55-59.

Contrasts the scores of inner-city and suburban ninth graders on a standardized occupational preference test in order to determine the relationship of social status and sex to guidance counseling. Results show that the socioeconomic status influence was greater than sex, with the inner-city students more concerned with work environments and the suburban students scoring higher on interpersonal satisfaction.

317 Skipper, Charles E. "Personal Characteristics of Adolescents with Average Intellectual Ability in a High Ability Suburban School District." CLEARINGHOUSE 50 (December 1976): 166-67.

Examines the influences of intellectual competition on the self-esteem of adolescents of average intellectual ability attending a high-ability suburban high school where there is strong pressure to achieve and go on to college. Comparisons of scores on standardized achievement and personality tests indicate that average-ability females are more adversely affected than average-ability males, and that both sexes tend to be more stubborn, insecure, defensive, and unambitious.

318 Stevens, A. Jay. "The Acquisition of Participatory Norms: The Case of Japanese and Mexican-American Children in a Suburban Environment." WESTERN POLITICAL QUARTERLY 28 (June 1975): 281-95.

Describes variations found in surveying Japanese-American, Chicano, and Anglo children in a Los Angeles suburb on measures of political efficacy, civic duty, and personal competence. Concludes that the suburban environment does not encourage the political acculturation of minority children.

319 Tallman, Irving. "Working-Class Wives in Suburbia: Fulfillment or Crisis?" JOURNAL OF MARRIAGE AND THE FAMILY 31 (February 1969): 65-72.

Tallman, Irving, and Morgner, Ramona. "Life-Style Differences among Urban and Suburban Blue-Collar Families." SOCIAL FORCES 48 (March 1970): 334-48.

The social and familial consequences of moving to the suburbs are the focus of work by Tallman and Morgner on blue-collar workers in the Minneapolis-St. Paul metropolitan area. Their results show that blue-collar suburbanites are more likely than their city counterparts to adopt middle-class lifestyles and that the move adversely affects family life, particularly in the destruction of the social relationships which support working-class women.

320 Wilkes, Paul. TRYING OUT THE DREAM. Philadelphia: Lippincott, 1975.

A journalistic account of life of an "average American family" in the suburbs. Wilkes lived with the family for a year and reports on its successes and failures, its trials and joys. The book treats the family members as individuals and explores each in his or her family and community environment.

321 Winch, Robert F.; Greer, Scott; and Blumberg, Rae Lesser. "Ethnicity and Extended Familism in an Upper-Middle Class Suburb." AMERICAN SOCIOLOGICAL REVIEW 32 (April 1967): 265-72.

Extends previous work on the relationships between familism and ethnicity, confirming, through the use of three new indexes, that Jews are more familistic than Christians. Finds extended familism to be a variable intervening between ethnicity and migration.

322 Zelan, Joseph. "Does Suburbia Make a Difference." In URBANISM IN WORLD PERSPECTIVE, edited by Sylvia Fleis Fava, pp. 401-8. New York: Crowell, 1968.

Author sought to test thesis that suburban children are less intellectual or oriented toward the arts than children from other sources. Secondary analysis of NORC survey of recent college graduates does not confirm the initial hypothesis. Further analysis of why some choose to live in suburbia and others do not places primary emphasis on community of origin: people who have lived in suburbia are oriented toward suburbia.

323 Zschock, Dieter K. "Black Youth in Suburbia." URBAN AFFAIRS QUARTERLY 7 (September 1971): 61-74.

General descriptive study of the lifestyle and problems of black youths in Nassau and Suffolk counties, New York, emphasizing their economic problems and concluding with several recommendations for alleviating the situation.

C. RELIGION

324 Carlos, Serge. "Religious Participation and the Urban-Suburban Continuum." AMERICAN JOURNAL OF SOCIOLOGY 75 (March 1970): 742-59.

Extends previous work on the influence of the urban environment on religious practices into suburbia. Results from a survey of Montreal-area Catholics indicates that with increased distance from the city center, the level of church attendance increases but the proportion of churchgoers engaging in other devotional religious practices decreases. Author attributes this to suburbanites' need for community identification and integration.

325 Goldstein, Sidney. "The Changing Socio-Demographic Structure of an
     American Jewish Community." JEWISH JOURNAL OF SOCIOLOGY 8
     (June 1966): 11-30.

     Provides information regarding the migration of Jews to the
     suburbs during the decade of the 1950s.

326 Gordon, Albert I. JEWS IN SUBURBIA. Boston: Beacon Press, 1959.

     Ringer, Benjamin B. THE EDGE OF FRIENDLINESS. New York: Basic Books,
     1967.

     Sklare, Marshall, and Greenblum, Joseph. JEWISH IDENTITY ON THE
     SUBURBAN FRONTIER. New York: Basic Books, 1967.

     The twenty years immediately following World War II saw the
     creation of a number of ethnic suburbs--suburbs dominated by
     one immigrant or religious group. The creation of Jewish sub-
     urbs and the movement of significant numbers of Jews into pre-
     viously gentile suburban communities challenged the WASP
     image of suburbia and at the same time added major new di-
     mensions to traditional Jewish-Protestant and Jewish-Catholic
     relations.

     Gordon in his JEWS IN SUBURBIA provided one of the earliest
     serious sociological portraits of this phenomenon. Writing in
     the late 1950s, Gordon identifies eighty-nine suburbs with high
     Jewish concentration. After describing generally the suburban-
     ization of American Jews, he looks at seven communities in
     particular. Family life, the synagogue, and ritual are studied.
     In closing, Gordon speculates on the frustrations and satisfac-
     tions which may influence both lifestyle and religious practice
     of Jewish people caught up in the suburban migration.

     JEWISH IDENTITY ON THE SUBURBAN FRONTIER and its com-
     panion THE EDGE OF FRIENDLINESS, sponsored by the Ameri-
     can Jewish Committee, are reports of field work in a midwes-
     tern suburb labeled "Lakeville." JEWISH IDENTITY covers
     much the same concerns treated by Gordon, while THE EDGE
     OF FRIENDLINESS concentrates on Jewish-gentile relations in
     the suburban context. Together they stand as a massive socio-
     logical case study, done with thoroughness and care and re-
     ported in a most professional manner. They are major contri-
     butions to the sociology of American religions. In this same
     series: Marshall Sklare, NOT QUITE AT HOME (New York:
     Institute of Human Relations Press, 1969).

     On the politics of Jews in suburbia, see Davidowicz, Lucy S.,
     and Goldstein, Leon J. "Jewish Voting Behavior." In POLI-
     TICS IN A PLURALIST DEMOCRACY (New York: Institute
     of Human Relations Press, 1963).

327   Schroeder, W. Widick, et al.   SUBURBAN RELIGION. Chicago: Center
      for the Scientific Study of Religion, 1974.

      There are very few serious sociological studies of religious ac-
      tivity in the suburbs. SUBURBAN RELIGION by Schroeder and
      his associates is a singular exception. Based on surveys with
      Protestant (white and black), Catholic, and Jewish lay persons
      and religious professionals in three south Chicago suburbs, this
      book describes the organizational patterns, activities, and per-
      sonal attitudes of suburban residents.

      First SUBURBAN RELIGION identifies "privatism" as a basic
      principle of American, but especially suburban, religion. By
      this the authors mean the overriding dominance of the congre-
      gational pattern of church policy, of each local church as a
      voluntary association of members, and of the tolerance of the
      private religious values or attitudes of each local member. At
      the same time, the authors note the pattern of suburban religion
      --denominationalism--is closely limited to the ethnic back-
      ground and socioeconomic status of various suburban residents.

      Earlier, more speculative treatments of related topics include
      the following:

          Shippey, Frederick A. PROTESTANTISM IN SUB-
          URBAN LIFE. New York: Abington Press, 1964.
          Winter, Gibson. THE SUBURBAN CAPTIVITY OF
          THE CHURCHES. Garden City, N.Y.: Doubleday,
          1961.
          Greeley, Andrew M. THE CHURCH AND THE SUB-
          URBS. New York: Sheed and Ward, 1959.

D. CRIME

328   Boggs, Sarah L. "Formal and Informal Crime Control: An Exploratory
      Study of Urban, Suburban, and Rural Orientations." SOCIOLOGICAL
      QUARTERLY 12 (Summer 1971): 319-27.

      Comparative study of central-city and suburban attitudes re-
      garding crime, crime prevention, and police protection.

329   Conklin, John E. "Dimensions of Community Response to the Crime Problem."
      SOCIAL PROBLEMS 18 (Winter 1971): 373-85.

      Investigates the relationship between perceptions of crime and
      individuals' attitudes and behavior in two communities, one a
      low crime suburban community, and one a high crime urban
      community, in the same unnamed metropolitan area. Findings
      show substantial differences in perception of local crime rates--
      differences which were not due to socioeconomic differences.
      The urban sample perceived higher crime rates, felt less safe,

was less trustful of others, had less positive feelings for the
community, and had stronger relationships between their perception of crime and the dimensions of their response. Conklin
observed that community life was affected only after perception of a certain level of crime had passed.

330   Conklin, John E., and Bittner, Egon. "Burglary in a Suburb." CRIMI-
       NOLOGY 11 (August 1973): 206-32.

       General description of the incidence of burglary in a north-
       eastern community.

331   Cowan, Ronald A.; Davis, James R.; and Frumkin, R.M. "Social Class
       and Drug Use among Metropolitan Hinterland High School Students."
       PSYCHOLOGICAL REPORTS 31 (October 1972): 387-90.

       Challenges commonly held assumptions that low social class is
       related to greater drug use, earlier use, and worse relations
       with parents, with a presentation of results from a survey of
       386 students in three different high schools in Oakland County
       (Detroit), Michigan. The upper middle-class suburban high
       school had the greatest incidence of drug use, while there
       were not significant differences between a lower middle-class
       suburban high school and a lower middle-class semirural high
       school.

332   Freeman, Beatrice, and Savastano, George. "The Affluent Youthful Of-
       fender." CRIME AND DELINQUENCY 16 (July 1970): 264-72.

       Study of the social psychology of young male suburban delin-
       quents and their families. Thirty cases in Nassau County,
       New York, were examined in detail over a two-year period.
       All of the families were middle class, had the child's natural
       parents living together, and had no previous family contact
       with law enforcement officials. Findings emphasize family in-
       fluence and conditions leading to criminal behavior.

333   Gitchoff, G. Thomas. KIDS, COPS, AND KILOS. San Diego, Calif.:
       Master-Westerfield Publishing Co., 1969.

       Investigation of youth and delinquency in an upper middle-class
       suburb of San Francisco. The author examines the values of
       young people during the 1960s and illustrates their frustrations
       with suburban life and the dominant American culture. Drug
       use, "dropping-out," and political activism are three mani-
       festations of this dissatisfaction explored. Given the changes
       which have occurred since the book was written, the findings
       may be quite dated.

334   Katz, Michael. "Violence and Civility in a Suburban Milieu." JOURNAL
      OF POLICE SCIENCE AND ADMINISTRATION 2 (September 1974): 239-49.

      Descriptive and analytical treatment of police violence in a
      suburban environment. Author finds some violence provoked
      by citizen initiative in citizen-police environment. However,
      he concludes that violence is neither a necessity nor a promi-
      nent feature of police work in the community studied.

335   Loth, David. CRIME IN THE SUBURBS. New York: William Morrow, 1967.

      According to newspaper accounts and official police statistics,
      suburbia is experiencing a significant increase in crime. Theft,
      robbery, assault, murder, delinquency, and drug use all are
      on the rise. By contrast, there is little or no increase in
      social science attention to this problem.

      In 1967 Loth published his descriptive overview of crime in
      the suburbs. Loth's material came from interviews with police
      chiefs and other observers around the country. Besides the
      obvious categories of criminal behavior, the author discusses
      both white-collar crime and organized crime. This book pro-
      vides the general reader with a good survey of conditions dur-
      ing the 1960s.

336   Senna, Joseph; Rathus, Spencer A.; and Siegel, Larry. "Delinquent Be-
      havior and Academic Investment among Suburban Youth." ADOLESCENCE
      9 (Winter 1974): 481-94.

      Investigates the relationship between school performance and
      delinquency in middle-class adolescents in a New York City
      suburb and finds no generalized delinquency factor.

337   Stein, Kenneth B.; Soskin, William F.; and Korchin, Sheldon J. "Drug
      Use among Disaffected High School Youth." JOURNAL OF DRUG EDU-
      CATION 5, no. 3 (1975): 193-203.

      Study of drug use among disaffected students in three different
      high schools--public urban, public suburban, and private resi-
      dential--in the San Francisco Bay area. Urban and suburban
      disaffected students used more drugs than their respective matched
      controls.

338   Sundeen, Richard A., and Mathieu, James. "The Fear of Crime and Its
      Consequences among Elderly in Three Urban Communities." GERON-
      TOLOGIST 16 (June 1976): 211-19.

      Results of a comparative study of attitudes held by the elderly
      regarding their fear of crime. Patterns were contrasted among
      Los Angeles census tracts, a suburban city, and a distant re-
      tirement community. Fear of crime and protective action taken

were highest in the city and lowest in the retirement community.
Even in the suburb considerable concern was manifested and
protective activity undertaken.

339   Tec, Nechama. GRASS IS GREEN IN SUBURBIA. Roslyn Heights, N.Y.:
       Libra Publishers, 1974.

       Sociological study of drug use--particularly marijuana--among
       suburban youth. Family experiences, high school environment,
       and peer group pressures are all explored as related causes of
       marijuana use. The author's emphases are primarily on drugs
       and youth rather than the suburban dimensions of their envi-
       ronment.

340   Tobias, Jerry J. "The Affluent Suburban Male Delinquent." CRIME AND
       DELINQUENCY 16 (July 1970): 273-79.

       Survey of 100 suburban offenders and comparison with similar
       group of urban offenders. Article emphasizes the prevalence
       of certain crimes among suburban offenders.

341   Viano, Emilio C. "Growing Up in an Affluent Society--Delinquency and
       Recidivism in Suburban America." JOURNAL OF CRIMINAL JUSTICE 3
       (Fall 1975): 223-36.

       Challenges traditional assumptions of juvenile justice with a
       study of suburban juvenile delinquents. The study finds no
       relationship between the juveniles' dispositions on criminal
       charges and their recidivism rates.

342   Walsh, Joseph A., and Witte, Pamela G. "Police Training in Domestic
       Crisis: A Suburban Approach." COMMUNITY MENTAL HEALTH JOUR-
       NAL 11 (Fall 1975): 301-6.

       Descriptive study of police encounters with domestic crises in
       several western Chicago suburbs.

E. RACIAL ATTITUDES

343   Elman, Richard M. ILL-AT-EASE IN COMPTON. New York: Pantheon,
       1967.

       Journalistic description of a lower middle-class suburb, half
       black and half white, in which it is difficult to separate the
       suburban, black, lower middle-class, and local factors in-
       fluencing the behavioral patterns pictured.

344   Engel, James F., and Blackwell, Roger D. "Affluent Suburbia and the Negro Neighbor." OHIO STATE UNIVERSITY BULLETIN OF BUSINESS RESEARCH 43 (October 1968): 1, 8-9.

_____. "Attitudes of Affluent Suburbia toward the Negro Neighbor." MICHIGAN STATE UNIVERSITY BUSINESS TOPICS 17 (Autumn 1969): 42-49.

Survey of 385 residents of Upper Arlington, a suburb of Columbus, Ohio, regarding their views of racial integration. Results showed generally positive or neutral attitudes toward residential integration by middle-class blacks. Education level appeared as a major factor influencing receptivity to black neighbors.

345   Hamilton, David L., and Bishop, George D. "Attitudinal and Behavioral Effects of Initial Integration of White Suburban Neighborhoods." JOURNAL OF SOCIAL ISSUES 32 (Spring 1976): 47-67.

Investigates the racial dimension of white suburban home owners' response to the initial integration of their previously all-white neighborhoods. Unique methodological features of the study include indirect measurements of behavior and attitude, interviews both before and after the new families' arrival, and the use of a control group of white families living near a recently arrived white family. Results from a test in the New Haven suburbs indicated that residents do react quite differently to new black and white families but that after a year the level of negative comments and expressions of symbolic racism declines.

346   Orbell, John, with Sherrill, Kenneth S. "Racial Attitudes and the Metropolitan Context: A Structural Analysis." PUBLIC OPINION QUARTERLY 33 (Spring 1969): 46-54.

In a test of the influence of residence on racial attitudes in the Columbus, Ohio, metropolitan area, authors found no significant differences in racial hostility by any individual status variable or by any aggregate variable treated separately. Whites in high-status white-only areas were equal in hostility to whites in low-status areas close to blacks.

347   Warren, Donald I. "Age Group Response to Race Tension: Survey Data from Post-Riot Detroit Suburbs." SOCIOLOGICAL SYMPOSIUM, no. 3 (Fall 1969): 151-57.

_____. "Community Dissensus: Panic in Suburbia." In A CITY IN RACIAL CRISIS, edited by Leonard Gordon, pp. 120-45. Dubuque, Iowa: William C. Brown Publishers, 1971.

_____. "Suburban Isolation and Race Tension: The Detroit Case." SOCIAL PROBLEMS 17 (Winter 1970): 324-39.

Warren reports the results of a survey of Detroit suburbanites' attitudes regarding the 1967 civil disturbance in Detroit. Most significant conclusions: a high degree of informational distortion characterizes white suburbanites' knowledge of the black community; socioeconomic levels affect suburbanites' attitudes toward the civil disturbance; suburban communities create their own isolated worlds which residents do not view as satellites of the central city; whites tend to attribute the cause of the riots to agitators, in contrast to blacks, who point to social forces or police abuses; the degree of racial tension in a suburb is related to the extent of anxiety about future race riots and support for reducing tension.

348 Zeul, Carolyn R., and Humphrey, Craig R. "The Integration of Black Residents in Suburban Neighborhoods: A Reexamination of the Contact Hypothesis." SOCIAL PROBLEMS 18 (Spring 1971): 462-74.

Authors examine the process of isolated black families moving into white neighborhoods and the subsequent social integration by surveying fifty housewives in an unnamed suburb. Findings demonstrate that cosmopolitanism of upper middle-class whites is unrelated to contact with blacks.

X. RACE, HOUSING, AND ZONING

349 Alexander, Ernest R. "Goal Setting and Growth in an Uncertain World: A Case Study of a Local Community Organization." PUBLIC ADMINIS-TRATION REVIEW 36 (March–April 1976): 182-91.

Case study of a neighborhood renewal project in the satellite city of Racine, Wisconsin.

350 Babcock, Richard F., and Bosselman, Fred P. EXCLUSIONARY ZONING. New York: Praeger, 1973.

General review of zoning and its impact on metropolitan housing patterns. Little explicit attention to suburbs per se.

351 Bergman, Edward M. ELIMINATING EXCLUSIONARY ZONING. Cambridge, Mass.: Ballinger, 1974.

Major empirical study of exclusionary zoning, its consequences, and its possible correction. Through the study of six suburban communities outside Philadelphia, the author develops a set of standards by which local zoning ordinances might be evaluated-- that housing be allowed to insure that workers in commercial and industrial areas can reside where they work. His analysis of the six communities encompasses a detailed look at their zoning ordinances, the impact of the ordinances on housing prices, the income capacity of local workers to meet local housing prices, and the econometric development of his standards for evaluating such ordinances.

352 Bernstein, Samuel J., and Mellon, W. Giles. "Stabilizing the Metropolis through Penetrating Suburban Neighborhoods: An Analytical Systems Approach." JOURNAL OF ENVIRONMENTAL SYSTEMS 1 (March 1971): 47-66.

Presents quantitative approach for analyzing the consequences of relocating poor minority group members from central-city ghettos into suburbs.

353 Danielson, Michael N. THE POLITICS OF EXCLUSION. New York: Columbia University Press, 1976.

A thorough, critical analysis of the question of access for the poor and other minorities to American suburbia. The basic orientation--an explicit antiexclusionary point of view--is evident from the title. Danielson assumes what an "open society" ought to be and builds on that foundation. Aside from the author's perspective, the book presents an extremely detailed discussion of existing conditions, the attacks against those conditions, and the suburban response.

Among the topics covered are the city-suburban class and race divisions, the political autonomy of suburbs, zoning, exclusion of subsidized housing, the limited political power of those excluded, the actions of courts, inaction at the state and national levels, and the "fair share" concept.

This is an excellent summary of the open access issue in suburbia. After a full exploration of the subject, Danielson is pessimistic about the prospects of change in the near future. A summary is presented in "The Politics of Exclusionary Zoning in Suburbia." POLITICAL SCIENCE QUARTERLY 91 (Spring 1976): 1-18.

354 Davidoff, Paul, and Davidoff, Linda. "Opening the Suburbs." SYRACUSE LAW REVIEW 22 (1971): 509-36.

Examines the tax consequences of exclusionary zoning and the other arguments used to support such suburban governmental policies.

355 Davidoff, Paul; Davidoff, Linda; and Gold, Neil Newton. "Suburban Action: Advocate Planning for An Open Society." JOURNAL OF THE AMERICAN INSTITUTE OF PLANNERS 36 (January 1970): 12-21.

Authors provide a general analysis of the metropolitan housing situation and the resulting racial patterns. They suggest housing desegregation as the best means for solving major urban problems and coping with the issues of poverty and unemployment. Advocacy planning and court challenges are proposed to change suburban conditions and to allow for metropolitan desegregation. A highly influential article which provided the basis for court activity in New Jersey for several years.

356 Davidoff, Paul, and Gold, Neil Newton. "Exclusionary Zoning." YALE REVIEW OF LAW AND SOCIAL ACTION 1 (Winter 1970): 56-63.

Further development of arguments presented in the "Suburban Action" article above.

357   DeVise, Pierre.   "Suburbs and Expressways, Barriers in Urban America."
      FOCUS/MIDWEST 9, no. 61 (1974):   10-18.

      Descriptive discussion of housing opportunities for minorities in
      the Chicago metropolitan area.

358   Downs, Anthony.   OPENING UP THE SUBURBS.   New Haven, Conn.:
      Yale University Press, 1973.

      Glazer, Nathan.   "On 'Opening Up' the Suburbs."   PUBLIC INTEREST,
      no. 37, Fall 1974, pp. 89-111.

      Downs's basic argument is that America's urban problems can
      be corrected only by providing both occupational and residen-
      tial access to the suburbs for inner-city populations.   The au-
      thor begins by reviewing the "trickle-down" process of American
      housing.   He argues that the process does not really work uni-
      formly as prescribed and, in any case, leaves the poor not
      simply with lower-cost housing but also with the poorest hous-
      ing in the worst condition concentrated in the worst areas.
      Thus, while serving the majority relatively well, the process
      is disastrous for the rest.

      Downs reviews the economic and racial differences between
      central cities and suburbs and the growing dominance of the
      suburbs.   He concludes that the economic future lies in the
      suburbs and that if minority populations are to take part in
      future economic benefits, they will have to be assured access
      to the suburbs.   After summarizing the expected benefits from
      opening up the suburbs, Downs considers the problems and
      opposition which would arise from a concentrated effort in
      this direction.   To overcome these difficulties, he generates
      a strategy based on a crucial assumption: the issues of racial
      integration versus class integration must be separated and class
      dominance in suburban neighborhoods must be preserved for
      present suburban residents to accept the proposal.   Thus, a
      quota system is devised.   Most of the rest of the book explains
      the Downs strategy, considers likely arguments against that
      strategy, and asserts the need to act in this arena.

      OPENING UP THE SUBURBS is a major analytical contribution
      in the newly burgeoning field of suburban-oriented public policy.

      In a critical analysis of Downs's theories, Glazer discusses the
      factual, racial, and policy issues raised.   Glazer does not
      believe that the magnitude of segregation is as great as is
      assumed by most or that the economic welfare of blacks would
      necessarily be improved by integrating the suburbs.   He is
      doubtful about the need for the "degree of heroism" called for
      by Downs because of the steady progress in integration already
      occurring, the impossibility of a successful public policy for
      the poor, and the extensive resistance encountered by imposed
      integration programs.

359 Grodzins, Morton. THE METROPOLITAN AREA AS A RACIAL PROBLEM.
     Pittsburgh: University of Pittsburgh Press, 1958.

> This extremely short book is a classic. Grodzins, analyzing
> population trends from 1940 to 1950, correctly foresaw the
> polarization of the metropolitan area into black central cities
> and white suburbs. He pinpointed the costs of suburban hous-
> ing and social antagonisms as the primary causes of these con-
> ditions. Grodzins proposed several solutions to the problem
> including (1) creating a free real estate market, (2) controlled
> quotas for minorities in local neighborhoods, (3) attracting
> white suburbanites back to the central cities, and (4) the sub-
> urbanization of the black middle class. This is a highly per-
> ceptive, timely little volume.

360 Gruen, Nina Jaffe, and Gruen, Claude. LOW AND MODERATE IN-
     COME HOUSING IN THE SUBURBS. New York: Praeger, 1972.

> This book is a research report done for the Miami Valley
> (Ohio) Regional Planning Commission by Gruen Gruen Asso-
> ciates. It is made up of the results from four distinct surveys--
> one of low- and moderate-income city residents, the second
> of Dayton area suburbanites, the third of local public officials,
> and the fourth a mini-survey of residents living in integrated
> neighborhoods around the country. The book closes with a
> general discussion of public housing policy and recommenda-
> tions for change.
>
> The low- and moderate-income survey consists of responses by
> 214 persons living in Dayton, Ohio, split 54 percent white
> and 46 percent black. People were asked their preferences
> for housing type (single-family, low-rise, and high-rise) resi-
> dential neighborhood situation, and racial integration versus
> segregation. Not surprisingly, interviewees favored single-
> family and low-rise to high-rise structures. However, of con-
> siderable importance was the finding that blacks preferred their
> own neighborhood (61 percent) to suburban locations (34 per-
> cent). Separate neighborhoods--defined economically--were
> strongly favored, while racially integrated neighborhoods were
> the top choice of all except white families with husbands present.
>
> The report on suburban attitudes went much further than that
> described above. About 200 suburbanites were questioned on
> their perceptions of the impact of various types of housing
> construction on existing neighborhoods, on attitudes toward the
> consequences of minority populations within a neighborhood,
> and on their reactions to different housing programs.
>
> Public officials were generally negative on the desirability of
> multifamily dwellings as residences and minority or disadvan-
> taged peoples as residents, but were rather positive toward
> housing programs.

In sum, the book provides some important information about suburban attitudes and about current issues focusing on future suburban development.

361 Guest, Avery M., and Weed, James A. "Ethnic Residential Segregation: Patterns of Change." AMERICAN JOURNAL OF SOCIOLOGY 81 (March 1976): 1088-111.

Traces patterns of ethnic residential segregation in Cleveland, Boston, and Seattle in order to determine if such segregation is increasing or decreasing in metropolitan areas, if it is related to social status differences between ethnic groups, and if ethnic groups are spatially distributed around the central business district according to Ernest W. Burgess's hypothesis of dispersal over time. (See Burgess's "The Growth of the City: An Introduction to a Research Project." THE CITY, edited by Robert E. Park, Ernest W. Burgess, and Robert D. McKenzie. Chicago: University of Chicago Press, 1925.) Analysis of census data shows the tenacious and pervasive nature of ethnic segregation, the at least moderate relation of shifts in segregation between 1930 and 1970 to differences in group status levels, and no clear pattern of centralization or decentralization of ethnic groups.

362 Haar, Charles M., and Iatridis, Demetrius S. HOUSING THE POOR IN SUBURBIA. Cambridge, Mass.: Ballinger, 1974.

Case studies from five Boston suburbs which illustrate the problems of trying to bring low and moderate cost housing to the suburbs. Four of the communities rejected these proposals. In one case, the program--with modest modification--was welcomed by local residents and public officials.

Each of the case studies is presented with meticulous thoroughness. Socioeconomic data are given. The project is described in detail with maps and quotes directly from the proposal. The politics of support and opposition are spelled out with care. The last two chapters of the book present materials illustrating American public policies affecting the introduction of low-cost housing into the suburbs.

Obviously intended for textbook use as well as the professional audience, the book is dominated by statistical data and documents, and each chapter closes with study or discussion questions.

For an early case study with much the same results, see Rosen, Harry, and Rosen, David, BUT NOT NEXT DOOR (New York: Ivan Obolensky, 1962).

363 Harrison, Bennett. "Suburbanization and Ghetto Dispersal: A Critique of the Conventional Wisdom." In CONTROVERSIES OF STATE AND LOCAL POLITICAL SYSTEMS, edited by Mavis Mann Reeves and Parris N. Glendening, pp. 401-8. Boston: Allyn and Bacon, 1972.

Author disputes the "ghetto dispersal" strategy as a means for achieving economic mobility for nonwhite workers. Summarized data from twelve SMSAs in 1965-66 indicate that minority residence in the suburbs does not necessarily produce access to suburban jobs for nonwhite populations.

364 Hughes, James W., ed. NEW DIMENSIONS IN URBAN PLANNING: GROWTH CONTROLS. New Brunswick, N.J.: Rutgers University Press, 1974.

This collection looks at the impact of court zoning decisions, community growth controls, and local politics on New Jersey suburbs in the mid-1970s. It includes the following:

Hughes, James W., and James, Franklin J. "The Dispersion of Employment: Planning Implications"
Burchell, Robert W.; Listokin, Daniel; and James, Franklin J. "Exclusionary Zoning: Pitfalls of the Regional Remedy"
Levin, Melvin R., and Rose, Jerome G. "The Suburban Land Use War: Skirmish in Washington Township, New Jersey"
Kirk, William. "Suburban Growth: Residential Pressures, Comment I"
Sears, Harry. "Suburban Growth: Residential Pressures, Comment II"
Hughes, James W. "The Fiscal and Social Impact of Alternative Forms of Housing"
James, Franklin J., and Windsor, Oliver Duane. "Local Land Use Controls in New Jersey: Their Effects of Housing Costs and Community Fiscal Advantage"
Listokin, Daniel. "The Changing Framework: Educational Funding Alternatives"
Baxter, Brian. "Local Fiscal Restraints: Municipal Behavior, Comment I"
Dorram, Peter. "Local Fiscal Restraints: Municipal Behavior, Comment II"
Abeles, Peter L. "Madison Township: Twenty Years too Late"
Rose, Jerome G. "Regulation of Population Growth and Distribution: A Review of the 1972-1973 Judicial Decisions"
_____. "Recent Decisions on Population Growth Control: The Belle Terre, Petaluma, and Madison Township Cases"

Wilentz, Robert N. "Growth, Zoning, and Land Use Controls: A Comment"

Greenberg, Michael R. "A Commentary on the Sewer Moratorium as a Piecemeal Remedy for Controlling Development"

Brail, Richard K. "The Implications of Air Quality Objectives for Metropolitan Growth"

Burchell, Robert W., and Hughes, James W. "Issues in Planned Unit Development"

Steinlieb, George S. "The Future of Housing in New Jersey"

Levin, Melvin R. "The Future of Land Use and Planning Education in New Jersey"

Gershen, Alvin E. "Exclusionary Zoning: Where the Arguments Fail"

365 Hughes, James W., and James, Franklin J. "Changing Spatial Distributions of Jobs and Residences." GROWTH AND CHANGE 6 (July 1975): 20-25.

Focuses on the capacity of mass transit to adjust to changing patterns of work trips within northeastern New Jersey and the nation and on how the issue is further aggravated by restrictive zoning practices. Authors find that the ideal location for industry is no longer the central city but rather along suburban freeways. They argue that suburban zoning restrictions lead to a mismatch between the capacity and the need for efficient transportation which in turn leads to dispersed residential demand and longer work trips.

366 Kain, John F. "Housing Segregation, Negro Employment and Metropolitan Decentralization." QUARTERLY JOURNAL OF ECONOMICS 82 (May 1968): 175-97.

Mooney, Joseph D. "Housing Segregation, Negro Employment and Metropolitan Decentralization: An Alternative Perspective." QUARTERLY JOURNAL OF ECONOMICS 83 (May 1969): 299-311.

Masters, Stanley H. "A Note on John Kain's 'Housing Segregation, Negro Employment and Metropolitan Decentralization.'" QUARTERLY JOURNAL OF ECONOMICS 83 (August 1974): 505-12.

Kain, John F. "Housing Segregation, Negro Employment and Metropolitan Decentralization: A Reply." QUARTERLY JOURNAL OF ECONOMICS 83 (August 1974): 513-19.

Kain hypothesizes that racial segregation in metropolitan housing markets affects the distribution of black employment, reduces black job opportunities, and has been seriously aggravated by postwar suburbanization of employment. He finds support for his hypotheses in an analysis of area traffic studies

Race, Housing, and Zoning

done in Detroit and Chicago in the 1950s. In their comments, Masters and Mooney each analyze data from several SMSAs and reach conclusions contradictory to Kain's. Kain responds by criticizing the measures used by Masters and Mooney and by stressing the constraints of high transportation costs.

367 Langendorf, Richard. "Residential Desegregation Potential." JOURNAL OF THE AMERICAN INSTITUTE OF PLANNERS 35 (March 1969): 90-95.

Author argues that in 1960 low-cost housing was available in the suburbs in sufficient quantity to increase markedly the minority population in those communities. Emphasizes segregation factors, not housing availability, as reason for metropolitan residential patterns.

368 Levin, Melvin R., and Rose, Jerome G. "The Suburban Land Use War: Skirmish in Washington Township, New Jersey." URBAN LAND 33 (May 1974): 14-18.

Case study of local political and judicial conflict over community zoning and the introduction of low-cost subsidized housing into the suburbs.

369 Listokin, David. FAIR SHARE HOUSING ALLOCATION. New Brunswick, N.J.: Rutgers University Press, 1976.

Provides a review of the need for low-cost housing in the suburbs and the rise of the "fair share" concept as a means for meeting that need. The process of generating a fair share plan is described and a number of working examples are provided. In addition, the book summarizes the existing fair share plans already in operation. Special attention is directed to the Dayton plan and other well-known proposals. The author concludes with a summary of the current status of the fair share concept and its prospects for the future.

370 Lustig, Morton, and Pack, Janet Rothenberg. "A Standard for Residential Zoning Based upon the Location of Jobs." JOURNAL OF THE AMERICAN INSTITUTE OF PLANNERS 40 (September 1974): 333-45.

Critique of restructive zoning codes in the suburbs. Authors suggest a standard for such codes based on the location of jobs within various communities. The proposed standard is then tested in Bucks County, Pennsylvania.

371 McFall, Trudy Parisa. "Housing Delivery on a Regional Basis." JOURNAL OF HOUSING 33 (October 1976): 427-30.

A short descriptive article on the role of the Minneapolis-St. Paul Metropolitan Council in providing redevelopment funds to

112

suburban communities. Both state and federal moneys are used. Article emphasizes importance of voluntary community participation in the program as well as the impact of the Metropolitan Council.

372 Marando, Vincent [L.]. "A Metropolitan Lower Income Housing Allocation Policy." AMERICAN BEHAVIORAL SCIENTIST 17 (September–October 1975): 75-103.

General discussion of the formulation and impact of a national policy by the U.S. Department of Housing and Development to develop metropolitan fair share housing plans through metropolitan councils of governments. Article quickly became dated and is primarily of interest for its historical content.

373 Marcus, Matityahu. "Racial Composition and Home Price Changes: A Case Study." JOURNAL OF THE AMERICAN INSTITUTE OF PLANNERS 34 (September 1968): 334-38.

Explores the impact of racial change in suburbs on housing values in surrounding communities. Plainfield, New Jersey, and neighboring areas used as a test case. Data suggest no significant relationship between racial change and decline in home values.

374 Moskowitz, David H. EXCLUSIONARY ZONING LITIGATION. Cambridge, Mass.: Ballinger, 1977.

This is not a book about suburbs. Rather it is an extremely detailed analysis of zoning and zoning litigation. The importance of this volume for suburbanists is in the cases themselves --most involve suburban communities. To the extent that zoning has shaped suburbia, this book describes one of the most basic forces operating in American metropolitan areas today. A must volume for the study of the whole suburban exclusion issue.

375 Phares, Donald. "Racial Change and Housing Values: Transition in an Inner Suburb." SOCIAL SCIENCE QUARTERLY 52 (December 1971): 560-73.

_____. "Racial Transition and Residential Property Values." ANNALS OF REGIONAL SCIENCE 5 (December 1971): 152-60.

Two articles which challenge the conventional assumption that residential property values decline as racial integration proceeds. Phares found no significant relationship between housing prices and racial transition in his study of University City, Missouri, a St. Louis suburb. Any differences observed among areas were eliminated in the long run.

376 Rabin, Yale. "Highways as a Barrier to Equal Access." ANNALS OF
THE AMERICAN ACADEMY OF POLITICAL AND SOCIAL SCIENCE 407
(May 1973): 63-77.

Argues that federal highway policy must be considered with
exclusionary zoning as the primary barrier to equal economic
access for minorities. Highways have increased residential and
occupational decentralization while, at the same time, their
design limits minority access to suburban jobs.

377 Roof, W. Clark, and Van Valey, Thomas L. "Residential Segregation
and Social Differentiation in American Urban Areas." SOCIAL FORCES
51 (September 1972): 87-91.

Methodological inquiry into the inconsistent results of studies
using residential segregation indexes. This study finds that
results vary with the use of SMSAs or central cities as the
base unit of analysis.

378 Rose, Jerome G., and Rothman, Robert E., eds. AFTER MOUNT LAUREL:
THE NEW SUBURBAN ZONING. New Brunswick, N.J.: Rutgers University Press, 1977.

Updates many topics covered in Hughes (item 364).

379 Rosser, Lawrence, and White, Beth. "An Answer to Housing Discrimination: the Need for a Unitary Marketing System." CIVIL RIGHTS DIGEST
7 (Winter 1975): 10-19.

Proposes new public policies and interim measures to open up
suburban housing to low- and moderate-income persons, including a clearinghouse on available suburban residential units and
a unitary metropolitan-wide real estate listing service.

380 Rubinowitz, Leonard S. "Exclusionary Zoning: A Wrong in Search of a
Remedy." UNIVERSITY OF MICHIGAN JOURNAL OF LAW REFORM 3
(1973): 625.

Examines exclusionary zoning cases, with a particular focus on
the problem of granting meaningful relief in such actions, and
draws an analogy between the duty to grant meaningful relief
in zoning cases with a similar duty in school desegregation
cases.

381 _____. LOW-INCOME HOUSING: SUBURBAN STRATEGIES. Cambridge, Mass.: Ballinger, 1974.

The author begins with a thorough analysis of the existence
and consequences of the exclusion of low-cost housing from
the suburbs. The barriers to the introduction of low-cost housing into the suburbs are identified. The bulk of the book examines

the public and private strategies which are being tried or might be tried to eliminate this condition. The lists are long and the treatment of each alternative is rather detailed. Among the public sector strategies discussed are inclusionary zoning by counties, state regulation of land use, state financing for and development of low-cost housing, the state as plaintiff in exclusion cases, federal housing programs, the location of federal facilities, and enforcement of federal civil rights legislation and regulations. Strategies in the private sector tend to concentrate on the initiation of litigation. However, Rubinowitz also discusses the corporate role in ending exclusionary practices and the task of building a suburban political constituency to support open housing.

This is an action-oriented book which at the same time provides solid documentation of efforts directed against suburban exclusion over the past decade.

382   Rubinowitz, Leonard S., and Dennis, Roger J.   "School Desegregation vs. Public Housing Desegregation: The Local School District and the Metropolitan Housing District."   URBAN LAW ANNUAL   10 (1975): 145-75.

Discussion of the lengthy litigation over the Chicago Housing Authority's policies, particularly the duty of federal courts to grant metropolitan-wide relief in housing discrimination cases, and a comparison of housing and school discrimination court cases.

383   Sager, Lawrence G.   "Tight Little Islands: Exclusionary Zoning, Equal Protection, and the Indigent."   STANFORD LAW REVIEW 21 (April 1969): 767-800.

A leading article which examines, from the perspective of the late 1960s, legal theories available to attack exclusionary zoning.

384   Schafer, Robert.   THE SUBURBANIZATION OF MULTIFAMILY HOUSING. Lexington, Mass.: D.C. Heath, 1974.

Presents a serious econometric analysis of the factors influencing the location of apartment units in suburbia, the kinds of people most likely to live in this type of housing, and the relation of work place to apartment development. Much of Schafer's analysis comes from data based on sixty different metropolitan areas. A detailed study of multifamily housing in the Boston SMSA concludes the work. Schafer's summary includes the prediction that suburban apartment construction will peak in the early 1980s and then begin to level off.

385   Schechter, Alan H.   "Impact of Open Housing Laws on Suburban Realtors."
        URBAN AFFAIRS QUARTERLY 8 (June 1973): 439-63.

        Based on a survey of realtors in two Boston suburbs, this study
        seeks to examine the impact of open housing legislation on
        realtor attitudes and on black access to the suburbs. The sur-
        vey explored levels of knowledge, the laws, realtor percep-
        tions of local problems, and attitudes toward the appropriate
        role of the government in local matters. The author concludes
        that enforcement is weak and as a result the impact of such
        laws is minimal.

386   Schexnider, Alvin J.   "Blacks, Cities, and the Energy Crisis." URBAN
        AFFAIRS QUARTERLY 10 (September 1974): 5-16.

        Speculates on the consequences of the continued shortage of
        gasoline for the integration of the suburbs, growth of black
        political power in the central cities, creation of rapid transit
        systems, and metropolitan development. Particularly concerned
        with reassessing the "hollow prize" thesis in terms of the energy
        crisis.

387   Sutker, Solomon, and Sutker, Sara Smith, eds. RACIAL TRANSITION IN
        THE INNER SUBURB. New York: Praeger, 1974.

        This collection of original essays focuses on the impact of
        racial transition on inner ring suburbs. The interest and tech-
        niques of the several authors vary. Included are the following
        essays:

                Sutker, Solomon. "New Settings for Racial Transition"
                Sutker, Solomon; Gilman, Richard C.; and Plax,
                    Karen A. "The Patterns and Concomitants of
                    Neighborhood Change in Two Inner Suburban Areas"
                Nourse, Hugh O., and Phares, Donald. "The Fil-
                    tering Process in the Inner Suburbs"
                Phares, Donald; McKenna, Joseph P.; and Werner,
                    Herbert D. "Neighborhood Change and Housing:
                    The Case of the Inner Suburbs"
                Sutker, Sara Smith. "The Journey to Work and a
                    New Residence in an Inner Suburb: Some Racial
                    Differences"
                _____. "Changes in Labor Force Performance for
                    Black New Resident Households in an Inner Suburb"

388   Stull, William J. "Community Environment, Zoning and the Market Value
        of Single-Family Homes." JOURNAL OF LAW AND ECONOMICS 18
        (October 1975): 535-57.

        Conducts an empirical test of the effect of zoning for various
        land uses on property values of nearby single-family homes in

forty suburbs of Boston in 1960. Using property values to measure preferences, author finds that home owners generally prefer
living in communities with a high proportion of single-family
homes to communities of mixed land uses. These home owners
did not perceive commercial, industrial, multifamily and vacant
land uses as equally undesirable. In addition, single-family
property values were found to be influenced by the community
equalized property tax rate, but public school quality was not
so influenced.

389 Taeuber, Karl E. "The Effect of Income Redistribution on Racial Residential Segregation." URBAN AFFAIRS QUARTERLY 4 (September 1968):
5-14.

General discussion of the spread of black families into the
suburbs, using the Cleveland area as an example. Author argues
that racial attitudes, not income differentials, best explain
segregation patterns.

390 Williams, Norman, Jr., and Norman, Thomas. "Exclusionary Land-Use
Controls: The Case of North-Eastern New Jersey." LAND USE CON-
TROLS QUARTERLY 4 (Fall 1970): 1-26.

Detailed land use and economic analysis of exclusionary zoning
in northeastern New Jersey designed to determine the amount
of land suitable and available for low- and moderate-income
housing.

XI. NEW TOWNS

391 Allen, Irvin Lewis, ed. NEW TOWNS AND THE SUBURBAN DREAM. Port Washington, N.Y.: Kennikat Press, 1977.

Arnold, Joseph L. THE NEW DEAL IN THE SUBURBS: A HISTORY OF THE GREENBELT TOWN PROGRAM, 1935-54. Columbus: Ohio State University Press, 1971.

Bailey, James, ed. NEW TOWNS IN AMERICA. New York: Wiley, 1973.

Brookes, Richard O[liver]. NEW TOWNS AND COMMUNAL VALUES. New York: Praeger, 1974.

Burby, Raymond J., and Weiss, Shirley F. NEW COMMUNITIES U.S.A. Lexington, Mass.: D.C. Heath, 1976.

Clapp, James A. NEW TOWNS AND URBAN POLICY. New York: Dunellen, 1971.

Golany, Gideon, and Walden, Daniel, eds. THE CONTEMPORARY NEW COMMUNITIES MOVEMENT IN THE UNITED STATES. Urbana: University of Illinois Press, 1974.

Lansing, John, et al. PLANNED RESIDENTIAL DEVELOPMENTS. Ann Arbor: University of Michigan Institute of Social Research, 1971.

Stein, Clarence S. TOWARD NEW TOWNS FOR AMERICA. Cambridge, Mass.: M.I.T. Press, 1957.

Watterson, Wayt T., and Watterson, Roberta S. THE POLITICS OF NEW COMMUNITIES. New York: Praeger, 1975.

New towns in one form or another have been part of American urban life since the first settlers arrived at the beginning of the seventeenth century. In the last fifty years new towns have taken on a new, more specific meaning. During these times the term "new town" has come to be used to describe consciously designed, newly constructed communities which provide both a more rural environment than the massive, congested cities and a more orderly and culturally richer environment than the typical sprawling suburb. Most--but not all-- such new towns have been developed near major central cities, like traditional suburbs, and have functioned very much like modern suburbs.

The twentieth-century new town movement got its start in the 1920s under the architectural leadership of Clarence Stein and Henry Wright. Radburn, New Jersey, was the first, and with federal funding the experiment continued through the depression years of the 1930s (see Stein, TOWARD NEW TOWNS FOR AMERICA, and Arnold, THE NEW DEAL IN THE SUBURBS).

Encouraged by the dual influences of the British and Scandinavian experiences and the American urban crisis, architects and policy planners turned again to the new town concept in the 1960s. Two private ventures, located in Reston, Virginia, and Columbia, Maryland, led the way. In 1968 Congress passed the New Communities Act to provide financial support for similar developments. For a summary of this movement up to 1970, see Clapp, NEW TOWNS AND URBAN POLICY, and Golany and Walden, CONTEMPORARY NEW COMMUNITIES MOVEMENT.

Burby and Weiss, NEW COMMUNITIES U.S.A., begins with a review of the new town movement in the United States. Most of the book is devoted to a study of thirteen privately developed American new towns, each paired for comparative purposes with a similar, nonplanned community nearby. More than 5,000 households were surveyed in these twenty-six communities and in several other new town and conventional locations. Questions focused on the kinds of people living in the various places, the reasons for moving to present residences, community services, and levels of public satisfaction. The authors also explored in some depth two new federally funded new towns--Jonathan, Minnesota, and Park Forest South, Illinois. The book closes with an evaluation of American new towns and a series of recommendations for public policy. This is truly an impressive book which adds considerably to our knowledge of nonplanned suburbs as well as planned new towns. See also Lansing, PLANNED RESIDENTIAL ENVIRONMENTS.

Two recent case studies illustrate the suburbanization of American new towns and discuss its implications. Watterson and Watterson, THE POLITICS OF NEW COMMUNITIES, looks at the San Antonio Ranch project, a new community under development about twenty miles northwest of downtown San Antonio. This study concentrates on the politics of land conversion on the urban frontier. Brooks, NEW TOWNS AND COMMUNAL VALUES, is an in-depth investigation of Columbia, Maryland-- its creation by the Rouse Corporation, its residents, and its internal conflicts. This case study, perhaps best of all, illustrates the inherent (at least in the United States) conflict between planning and local politics in the metropolitan context.

For architectural and design information about recent American

new towns, see Bailey, NEW TOWNS IN AMERICA. Allen,
NEW TOWNS AND THE SUBURBAN DREAM, is a reader dealing
with new towns and suburbia.

392   Popenoe, David. THE SUBURBAN ENVIRONMENT. Chicago: University
of Chicago Press, 1977.

A comparative study of life and residential conditions in Val-
lingby, Sweden (a new town suburb outside Stockholm), and
Levittown, Pennsylvania (a Levitt-built tract suburb outside
Philadelphia). The book contains an excellent introductory
essay covering the literature on American suburbia and new
town development overseas. The author concludes that the
Swedish model provides a direction which ought to be seriously
considered as an alternative to American patterns over the
past thirty years.

Appendix A

BIBLIOGRAPHIES, ABSTRACTS, AND INDEXES

The suburban literature, like all social science literature, does not stand still. Theories are constantly being retested and restated, new findings presented and analyzed, new books and articles generated and published. To gather the references for this bibliography, the authors used several standard library reference works and a few not so obvious means which can be employed by anyone to update our work.

1. To find books on suburbs, look in a library card catalog, CUMULATIVE BOOK INDEX, SUBJECT GUIDE TO BOOKS IN PRINT, and SUBJECT GUIDE TO FORTHCOMING BOOKS IN PRINT.

2. Articles in single-author works and anthologies can be gleaned from books found by the above method and in ESSAY AND GENERAL LITERATURE INDEX.

3. The following indexing and abstracting services were found to yield the most journal articles:

ABC POL SCI
AMERICA: HISTORY AND LIFE
ART INDEX
BUSINESS PERIODICALS INDEX
CURRENT INDEX TO JOURNALS IN EDUCATION
EDUCATION INDEX
GEO ABSTRACTS, Parts C, D, and F
HOUSING AND PLANNING REFERENCES
INDEX TO LEGAL PERIODICALS
JOURNAL OF ECONOMIC LITERATURE
POPULATION INDEX
PSYCHOLOGICAL ABSTRACTS
PUBLIC AFFAIRS INFORMATION SERVICE (PAIS)
READERS GUIDE TO PERIODICAL LITERATURE (useful for journalistic, nonscholarly articles only)
SOCIAL SCIENCES CITATION INDEX (both the Permuterm index and the citations)
SOCIAL SCIENCES INDEX
SOCIOLOGICAL ABSTRACTS

4. While the most productive terms to search under will vary from index to index, these terms and their variants should be consulted in every index: suburb, city, cities and towns, metropolitan, urban, urbanization, local government, municipal, residential mobility, rural-urban, migration, zoning, new towns, intrametropolitan. Sometimes it is best to scan entire sections of an index devoted specifically to urban studies, as in SOCIOLOGICAL ABSTRACTS or AMERICA: HISTORY AND LIFE.

5. A recent study of the distribution of journal articles on suburbs* showed that articles tend to concentrate in a few key journals. These are LAND ECO-NOMICS, URBAN AFFAIRS QUARTERLY, and JOURNAL OF THE AMERICAN INSTITUTE OF PLANNERS. Issues of these journals should be regularly scanned for relevant articles.

6. Journal advertising pages are a good place to look for announcements of recently published or forthcoming books on suburbs. Book reviews in scholarly journals are important for their critical analyses but often do not appear for several months after publication of the reviewed books. Book reviews of known titles may be located through BOOK REVIEW DIGEST and BOOK REVIEW INDEX.

7. The footnotes and bibliographies of books and journal articles are an important source of previous research on a particular topic. The process has been made considerably easier with the publication of SOCIAL SCIENCES CITATION INDEX, a reference work which operates on the presumption that most articles only cite other articles which are relevant to the topic discussed. Thus a suburban researcher could select a journal article from this bibliography and through the citation indexing process find more recently published articles which cite the original article and are therefore presumably on the same topic.

8. An essential starting point in searching for material on suburbs published before 1965 is a bibliography compiled by Louis H. Masotti and Deborah Ellis Dennis, SUBURBS, SUBURBIA AND SUBURBANIZATION: A BIBLIOGRAPHY, 2d ed. (Monticello, Ill.: Council of Planning Librarians, 1974). The bibliography is not annotated but contains references to the journalistic articles, dissertations, government documents, and ephemera omitted in this work.

---

*Deborah Ellis Dennis, "Bradford's Law of Scattering and the Journal Literature on Suburbs." Master's thesis, University of Chicago, 1976.

Appendix B
PERIODICALS WITH CONTENT RELEVANT TO
URBAN AND SUBURBAN AFFAIRS

In addition to the popular news weeklies, such as NEWSWEEK, TIME, and U.S. NEWS AND WORLD REPORT, there are a number of academic or professional journals with content relevant to urban and suburban affairs. The most significant are listed below and their contents are generally indexed by Public Affairs Information Service and the Social Science Index.

ADMINISTRATION AND SOCIETY. Beverly Hills, Calif.: Sage Publications, 1974-- . Quarterly. (Formerly JOURNAL OF COMPARATIVE ADMINISTRA-TION.)

AMERICAN COUNTY GOVERNMENT. Washington, D.C.: National Association of County Officials, 1935-- . Monthly.

AMERICAN JOURNAL OF POLITICAL SCIENCE. Detroit: Wayne State University Press, 1973-- . Quarterly.

AMERICAN POLITICAL SCIENCE REVIEW. Menasha, Wis.: George Banta Co., 1906-- . Quarterly.

AMERICAN POLITICS QUARTERLY. Beverly Hills, Calif.: Sage Publications, 1973-- . Quarterly.

AMERICAN SOCIOLOGICAL REVIEW. Menasha, Wis.: American Sociological Society, 1936-- . Bimonthly.

ANNALS. Philadelphia: American Academy of Political and Social Science, 1890-- . Annual.

THE BLACK SCHOLAR. San Francisco, Calif.: Black World Foundation, 1969-- . Monthly, except July and August.

BUREAUCRAT. Beverly Hills, Calif.: Sage Publications, 1972-- . Quarterly.

CITY. Washington, D.C.: Urban America, 1967-- . Annual.

COMPARATIVE URBAN RESEARCH. New York: City University of New York, Comparative Urban Studies Center, 1972-- . 2/year.

CONGRESSIONAL QUARTERLY WEEKLY REPORT. Washington, D.C.: Congressional Quarterly.

EDUCATION AND URBAN SOCIETY. Beverly Hills, Calif.: Sage Publications, 1968-- . Quarterly.

ENVIRONMENT AND PLANNING. London: Pion, 1969-- . Quarterly.

JOURNAL OF BLACK STUDIES. Beverly Hills, Calif.: Sage Publications, 1970-- . Quarterly.

JOURNAL OF POLITICS. Gainesville, Fla.: Southern Political Association, 1939-- . Quarterly.

JOURNAL OF REGIONAL SCIENCE. Philadelphia: Regional Science Research Institute, 1958-- . Biannual.

JOURNAL OF THE AMERICAN INSTITUTE OF PLANNERS. Cambridge, Mass.: American Institute of Planners, 1935-- . Quarterly.

JOURNAL OF URBAN ECONOMICS. New York: Academic Press, 1974-- . Quarterly.

LAW AND SOCIETY REVIEW. Denver, Colo.: Law and Society Association, 1966-- . Quarterly.

NATIONAL CIVIC REVIEW. Worcester, Mass.: National Municipal League, 1912-- . Frequency varies.

NATIONAL JOURNAL. Washington, D.C.: Center for Political Research, 1969-- . Weekly.

NATION'S CITIES. Washington, D.C.: National League of Cities, 1963-- . Quarterly.

THE PLANNER. London: Royal Town Planning Institute, 1973-- . 10/year.

POLICY AND POLITICS. London: Sage Publications, 1972-- . Quarterly.

POLICY SCIENCES. New York: American Elsevier, 1970-- . Quarterly.

POLICY STUDIES JOURNAL. Urbana: University of Illinois, 1972-- . Quarterly.

POLITICAL SCIENCE QUARTERLY. New York: Academy of Political Science, Columbia University, 1886-- .

POLITY. Amherst: University of Massachusetts, 1968-- . Quarterly.

PUBLIC ADMINISTRATION REVIEW. Washington, D.C.: American Society for Public Administration, 1940-- . Bimonthly.

PUBLIC AFFAIRS REPORT. Berkeley: Institute of Governmental Studies, University of California, 1960-- . Monthly.

PUBLIC FINANCE QUARTERLY. Beverly Hills, Calif.: Sage Publications, 1973-- .

THE PUBLIC INTEREST. New York: National Affairs, 1965-- . Quarterly.

PUBLIC MANAGEMENT. Chicago: International City Management Association, 1919-- . Monthly.

PUBLIUS. Philadelphia: Center for the Study of Federalism, Temple University, 1971-- . Frequency varies.

REVIEW OF BLACK POLITICAL ECONOMY. New York: Black Economic Research Center, 1970-- . Quarterly.

SOCIAL SCIENCE QUARTERLY. Austin: Southwestern Social Science Quarterly, University of Texas, 1919-- .

SOCIETY. Philadelphia: Transaction, 1972-- . Monthly.

URBAN AFFAIRS QUARTERLY. Beverly Hills, Calif.: Sage Publications, 1965-- .

URBAN LAWYER. Chicago: American Bar Association, 1969-- . Quarterly.

WESTERN POLITICAL QUARTERLY. Salt Lake City: Institute of Government, University of Utah, 1948-- .

AUTHOR INDEX

This index includes all authors, editors, compilers, and contributors to works cited in the text. Alphabetization is letter by letter. Numbers refer to entry numbers.

A

Abeles, Peter L. 364
Abler, Ronald 32
Adams, Charles 265
Adams, John S. 32, 33
Alexander, Ernest R. 349
Allen, Irving Lewis 391
Allensworth, Don T. 178
Altshuler, Alan 55
André, Carolyn D. 28
Andrew, Ralph 235
Anton, Thomas J. 34
Archer, R.W. 63
Armstrong, Regina Belz 83
Arnold, Joseph L. 391
Aronson, J. Richard 270
Aschmon, Frederick T. 21
Auld, D.A.L. 266

B

Babcock, Richard F. 26, 350
Bahl, Roy W. 251, 252
Bailey, James 391
Baker, Earl M. 15
Baldassare, Mark 291
Balkin, Esther 308
Barth, Ernest A.T. 206
Barton, Josef J. 26
Baxter, Brian 364

Beaton, W. Patrick 114
Bell, Charles G. 208
Bell, Wendell 16, 142
Berger, Bennett M. 7, 104
Bergman, Edward M. 351
Bernstein, Samuel J. 352
Berry, Brian J.L. 26, 28, 118, 215
Beyer, Glenn H. 8
Birch, David L. 24, 35, 64, 278, 292
Bish, Robert L. 279
Bishop, George D. 345
Bittner, Egon 330
Blackwell, Roger D. 344
Blase, Melvin G. 65
Bloomberg, Warner, Jr. 232
Blumberg, Leonard 156
Blumberg, Rae Lesser 321
Boelaert, Remi 253
Bogart, Leo 293
Boggs, Sarah L. 328
Borgatta, Edgar F. 10
Boskoff, Alvin 294
Bosselman, Fred P. 350
Bowman, John H. 262
Bowman, Lewis 174
Boyd, William L. 223
Bradford, Calvin P. 24
Bradford, David F. 276
Brail, Richard K. 364
Brazer, Marjorie Cahn 254

Author Index

Author Index

Hoover, Edgar M.   30, 46, 66
Horton, Frank E.   118
Hugg, Lawrence   159
Hughes, James W.   22, 24, 93, 364, 365
Humphrey, Craig R.   300, 348
Hushak, Leroy J.   70

I

Iannaccone, Laurence   224
Iatridis, Demetrius S.   362
Ippolito, Dennis S.   168, 174

J

Jackson, Kenneth T.   17, 47, 48, 79
Jackson, Robert Max   28
Jackson, Robin   16
James, Franklin J.   93, 364, 365
James, Gilbert   301
Jones, Joy K.O.   30
Jung, L. Shannon   302

K

Kain, John F.   94, 366
Kaiser, Edward J.   71, 72, 143
Kaplan, Samuel   17, 303
Kasarda, John D.   28, 49, 175, 261
Katz, Michael   334
Kaufman, Nathan B.   176
Kee, Woo Sik   262, 263
Kelejian, Harry H.   276
Kirk, William   364
Kirkpatrick, Samuel A.   179
Kirschenbaum, Alan   148
Klaff, Vivian Zelig   138
Knight, Richard V.   287
Koehler, Cortus T.   304
Komarovsky, Mirra   107
Koppleman, Lee K.   31
Korchin, Sheldon J.   337
Kramer, John   23, 161, 167
Krout, John A.   300

L

Ladd, Everett Carll   245
Lake, Robert W.   24

Lalli, Michael   156
Lamare, James   54
Lamb, Karl A.   177
Langendorf, Richard   367
Lansing, John   391
Lee, S. Young   122
Lehne, Richard   24, 219
Lekachman, Robert   31
LeMasters, E.E.   311
Leonard, William N.   16
Leshinski, Stephen   273
Levenson, Albert M.   30, 31
Levin, Melvin R.   364, 368
Levin, Sharon G.   264
Levine, Daniel U.   246, 312
Levine, Marvin   99
Lewis, George K.   84
Licht, M.   313
Lineberry, Robert L.   24
Linowes, R. Robert   78
Listokin, Daniel   364
Listokin, David   369
Logan, John R.   95
Long, Larry H.   28, 130
Loosley, Elizabeth W.   112
Lopata, Helena Z.   314
Lord, J. Dennis   247
Loth, David   335
Loveridge, Ronald O.   169
Lowi, Theodore J.   111
Lows, Raymond L.   234
Lundberg, George A.   107
Lustig, Morton   370
Lutz, Frank W.   224
Lyons, W.E.   198, 199, 200

M

McCausland, John L.   21
McDavid, James C.   201
McDonnell, William C.   186
McFall, Trudy Parisa   371
McInerny, Mary Alice   107
McKee, David L.   50
McKenna, Joseph P.   387
McKenzie, Robert D.   361
Manis, Jerome G.   80
Marando, Vincent L.   96, 202, 203, 372
Marcus, Matityaku   373

Author Index

Roof, W. Clark 377
Rose, Harold M. 164, 165, 166
Rose, Jerome G. 364, 368, 378
Rosen, David 362
Rosen, Harry 362
Ross, Philip 183
Rosser, Lawrence 379
Rothenberg, Jerome 286
Rothman, Robert E. 378
Rubin, Richard L. 210
Rubinowitz, Leonard S. 24, 26, 380, 381, 382

S

Sabagh, George 150
Sacks, Seymour 235, 268
Sagalyn, Lynne Beyer 115
Sager, Lawrence G. 383
Savastano, George 332
Schafer, Robert 384
Schechter, Alan H. 385
Schexnider, Alvin J. 386
Schiltz, Timothy 12
Schmid, A. Allan 74
Schnall, David J. 184
Schnidman, Frank 82
Schnore, Leo F. 27, 28, 30, 48, 132, 136, 137, 138, 139
Schroeder, W. Widick 327
Schuerman, Leo A. 141
Schultz, Stanley K. 79
Schuman, Howard 21
Schwartz, Barry 28
Schwartz, Eli 270
Schwartz, Joel 17
Schwartz, S.I. 68
Schwirian, Kent P. 51
Scott, Claudia D. 259
Scott, David W. 15
Scott, Thomas M. 24, 26
Sears, Harry 364
Seeley, John R. 106, 112
Senna, Joseph 336
Shappell, Dean L. 316
Sharp, Harry 28
Shepard, W. Bruce 205
Sherrill, Kenneth S. 346
Shippey, Frederick A. 327
Shipton, Robert 57

Sichel, Joyce L. 249
Siegel, Jay 151
Siegel, Larry 336
Siembieda, William J. 24, 163
Simons, Peter L. 100
Sims, R. Alexander 112
Sinclair, Robert 57
Singleton, Gregory H. 26
Skipper, Charles E. 317
Sklare, Marshall 326
Smith, Gerald H. 50
Smith, Joel 78, 140
Smith, Michael P. 229, 236
Smith, Robert 30
Smookler, Helene V. 24
Sobin, Dennis P. 4, 113
Soskin, William F. 337
Stanback, Thomas M. 287
Staub, William J. 65
Stegman, Michael A. 152
Stein, Clarence S. 391
Stein, Kenneth B. 337
Stephens, G. Ross 288
Sternlieb, George S. 24, 114, 115, 364
Stevens, A. Jay 318
Stockwell, Edward G. 123
Stonier, Charles E. 16, 58
Strong, Ann L. 75
Stuart, Darwin G. 59
Stull, William J. 388
Sundeen, Richard A. 338
Sunley, Emil M., Jr. 269
Sunshine, Morris 232
Sutker, Sara Smith 387
Sutker, Solomon 387

T

Taeuber, Karl E. 24, 389
Tallman, Irving 319
Tarver, James D. 153
Taylor, Graham Romeyn 107
Tec, Nechama 339
Teska, Robert B. 59
Thomas, Edward G. 315
Thompson, Wilbur R. 26
Tiebout, Charles M. 270, 271, 272, 273, 274, 275
Tobias, Jerry F. 340

TITLE INDEX

This index includes all books cited in the text. Articles and journals have not been included. Alphabetization is letter by letter. Numbers refer to entry numbers.

METROPOLITAN AREA INDEX

This index covers metropolitan areas discussed in the text in relation to suburbia.
Alphabetization is letter by letter. Numbers refer to entry numbers.

A

Atlanta 168, 236, 294
Augusta (Georgia) 200

B

Baltimore 186, 309
Birmingham 162
Boston 39, 60, 84, 242, 362, 384, 385, 388
Buffalo 147

C

Charlotte (North Carolina) 247
Chicago 15, 28, 29, 59, 87, 97, 111, 116, 118, 121, 142, 223, 226, 227, 228, 234, 314, 321, 327, 334, 342, 357, 362, 379
Cleveland 211
Columbus (Ohio) 70, 180, 181, 344

D

Dayton 360
Denver 67
Detroit 28, 38, 57, 84, 182, 202, 204, 217, 243, 266, 285, 291, 331, 347

G

Grand Rapids (Michigan) 26
Greensboro (North Carolina) 71

H

Harrisburg 270
Hartford 245

I

Indianapolis 26

J

Jacksonville (Florida) 24

K

Kalamazoo 80
Kansas City 65, 246

L

Lexington 63, 198, 199, 200
Los Angeles 24, 42, 54, 92, 141, 157, 177, 190, 192, 208, 304, 318, 338, 343

DATE DUE
